W9-CEK-225

SITTING IN,
STANDING UP

Leaders of the
Civil Rights Era

DIANE C. TAYLOR

EXPLORE QR CONNECTIONS!

You can use a smartphone or tablet app to scan the QR codes and explore more! Cover up neighboring QR codes to make sure you're scanning the right one. You can find a list of urls on the Resources page.

If the QR code doesn't work, try searching the internet with the Keyword Prompts to find other helpful sources.

🔍 civil rights leaders

Nomad Press

A division of Nomad Communications

10 9 8 7 6 5 4 3 2 1

This book was manufactured by CGB Printers, North Mankato, Minnesota, United States
November 2020, Job #1013835
ISBN Softcover: 978-1-61930-915-9
ISBN Hardcover: 978-1-61930-912-8

Educational Consultant, Marla Conn

Questions regarding the ordering of this book should be addressed to
Nomad Press
2456 Christian St., White River Junction, VT 05001
www.nomadpress.net

Printed in the United States.

Discover the **PASSION** and **CONVICTION** of the **1950s**, **'60s**, and **'70s!**

In *Changing Laws: Politics of the Civil Rights Era*, middle graders explore the key legislative and judicial victories of the era that spanned from 1954 to the early 1970s, including *Brown v. Board of Education*, the Civil Rights Act of 1964, the Voting Rights Act of 1965, and the Fair Housing Act of 1968, all of which couldn't have happened without the increased activism of the times. Kids explore how marches, demonstrations, boycotts, and lawsuits prodded local and state governments to examine the bigotry of their laws and the brutality of their oppression of Black citizens.

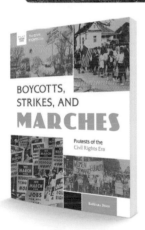

In *Boycotts, Strikes, and Marches: Protests of the Civil Rights Era*, readers 12 through 15 explore five groundbreaking protests that took place during the 1950s, 1960s, and early 1970s. Become immersed in the spirit of the Montgomery bus boycott, the draft card burning protests of the Vietnam War, the Delano grape strike and boycott, the first Gay Pride March, and the Women's Strike for Equality. Middle schoolers also learn about the conditions that prompted these demonstrations and how protest organizers used critical and creative thinking to surmount the challenges they faced to initiate meaningful change.

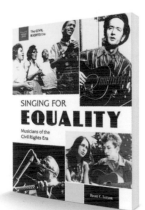

Singing for Equality: Musicians of the Civil Rights Era introduces middle graders to the history of the Civil Rights Movement and explores the vital role that music played in the tumultuous period of American history during the 1950s, '60s, and '70s.

The heart of the Civil Rights Movement beats in the music and musicians of the times, whose work was both an inspiration and a reflection of the changes happening in America and to its people. Bob Dylan, Mavis Staples and the Staple Singers, Sam Cooke, James Brown, and Nina Simone epitomized the passion and commitment shown by those involved in the movement, and portrayed the struggles encountered by an entire race of people with gritty beauty and moving calls to action and thought.

TABLE OF
CONTENTS

John Lewis

 Ella Baker

Fannie Lou
Hamer

Martin Luther
King Jr.

Glossary
—
Resources
—
**Selected
Bibliography**
—
Index
—

Thurgood Marshall

The March on Washington, 1963

WHO WILL LEAD US?

The Civil Rights Movement was a time when a great many people rose up and demanded change, the kind of change that would improve the lives of millions of people. It was a tumultuous, difficult time, but a crucial one in the history of the United States. It was the moment when the ideals outlined in the U.S. Constitution, that all are created equal, were held up to the bright light of societal scrutiny and found missing.

FASTFACTS

WHAT?
The Civil Rights Movement was a time when Black Americans demanded their full rights as citizens of the United States.

WHY?
African Americans in the United States had been denied many civil rights, such as the right to vote, to attend college, or to receive a fair trial in a court of law.

WHEN?
From the mid 1950s to early 1970s

HOW?
Leaders of the Civil Rights Movement inspired people across the country to work toward their goals of equality for all.

1

Do you feel as though your own civil rights are respected? If your high school grades are good enough, can you apply to any college you want? Do you look forward to one day voting in a presidential election? When you ride public transportation, do you take whatever seat is available? Do you feel safe in the presence of police officers?

If you answer "yes" to those questions, that means you feel you can pursue your goals and desires. You can participate in shaping your government and have nothing to fear from law enforcement.

If you answer "no" to those questions, that might mean you don't feel your civil rights are recognized.

You might not feel allowed to go to the college of your choice. You might not be allowed to vote. You might not be allowed to sit where you want on a bus, train, or airplane. The police might arrest you for no good reason. The color of your skin could make it hard for you to find a good job and a decent place to live.

Answering "no" to those questions might mean that your civil rights are not fully protected.

Word Power!

This book is packed with lots of new vocabulary! Try figuring out the meanings of unfamiliar words using the context and roots of the words. There is a glossary in the back to help you and Word Power check-ins for every chapter.

What Are Civil Rights?

The United States was founded on the idea that all people are created equal. Each year on the Fourth of July, we celebrate the 1776 signing of the Declaration of Independence. This is the document that laid the foundation for America to form a country separate from Great Britain. American colonists went to war against Great Britain in order to create a country where all citizens would be granted basic rights, such as "Life, Liberty and the pursuit of Happiness."

CIVIL RIGHTS TIMELINE

1955
People in Montgomery, Alabama, boycott the city's segregated bus system.

September 1957
Nine Black teenagers integrate all-white Central High School in Little Rock, Arkansas.

May 1960
Lunch counter sit-ins begin in Nashville, Tennessee.

Freedom for all was a bold idea. But it has never been an easy idea to put into practice. Even as the Declaration of Independence was being signed, for example, colonists owned slaves. Native Americans and African Americans had no civil rights at all.

Similarly, women were controlled by their fathers, husbands, or brothers. They were not allowed to own property, pursue an education or a career, or vote.

"Freedom is never really won. You earn it and win it in every generation."

Coretta Scott King (1927–2006), civil rights activist and wife of Martin Luther King Jr.

This 1819 painting by John Trumbull shows the drafting of the Declaration of Independence. Is it fair that there were no women, Black, Indigenous, or people of color there?

August 1963
The March on Washington sees more than 200,000 people rallying for civil rights.

1964
The Civil Rights Act of 1964 prohibits discrimination in public facilities and employment.

April 4, 1968
Martin Luther King Jr. is assassinated by James Earl Ray at the Lorraine Motel in Memphis, Tennessee.

April 11, 1968
The Civil Rights Act of 1968 outlaws discrimination in housing based on race, religion, or national origin.

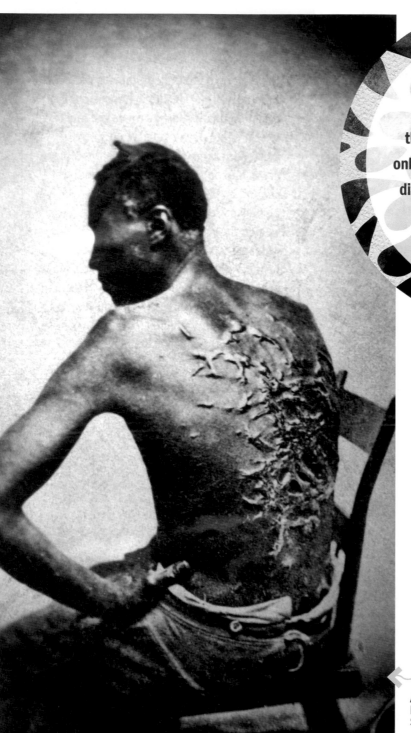

WONDER WHY?

Today's Black Lives Matter movement grows through marches and within online communities. How is this different from the Civil Rights Movement? Do you think the outcomes will be different?

Slavery was gone, but in its place was a system of customs and laws known as Jim Crow. The Jim Crow South was a segregated society. White and Black people lived totally separate and unequal lives. For example, they lived in separate neighborhoods, and the Black neighborhoods were always on the poor side of town.

They went to separate schools, and the Black schools were never as well funded as the white schools. Schools for Blacks sometimes even lacked indoor plumbing and heating.

A Black man bears the scars of the brutal beatings he received at the hands of white Southern slave masters.

Credit: McPherson and Oliver, working for Mathew Brady

They drank from separate public water fountains. One was labeled for "coloreds," a term once used for Black people that is now considered offensive. Another was labeled for "whites." It was a crime for a Black person to drink from a white person's water fountain. They used separate public bathrooms. As with the water fountains, they were labeled for "coloreds" and "whites."

If you visited a restaurant in the South in the first half of the twentieth century, you wouldn't see white and Black people sitting near each other. In fact, Black people couldn't even eat in the same restaurants as whites. Climb aboard a bus and white people would be sitting near the front, Black people in the back. If white people got on a bus and no seats were available, Black people were required to give up their seats. It was the law.

A Black man drinks from a segregated water fountain in 1939.

Credit: Russell Lee

THE ORIGIN OF JIM CROW

No one knows exactly how the term "Jim Crow" came to refer to segregation laws in the southern United States. During the late 1830s and early 1840s, Jim Crow was a Black character played by a white actor named Thomas D. Rice (1808–1860). Rice performed in blackface (this means he painted his face black) and played Jim Crow in a song-and-dance routine that made fun of Black people. Rice's Jim Crow routine was hugely popular with American audiences. At some point, the term "Jim Crow" moved out of the theater and into politics. By 1892, *The New York Times* was using "Jim Crow" as a political term in a story about segregated railroad cars in Louisiana.

Terrorizing the Black Population

Jim Crow laws were one tool that white people used to deny African Americans their civil rights. Terror was another. For Black people, being arrested for no offense could be the least of their concerns. Mobs of angry, violent white folks were far more dangerous.

In the decades after the Civil War, Southern whites formed racist groups that went beyond the law to ensure that Black people would never rise above a lowly station in life. The largest and most influential of these groups was the Ku Klux Klan (KKK). Members of the KKK included everyone from doctors and lawyers to policemen and mechanics, men and women alike. They banded together to use violence to oppress their Black neighbors.

It didn't take much to arouse the anger of the KKK. Members passed harsh judgment on anything they perceived as an insult toward them or other white people, especially women. A Black man might wake up the next night to find a large wooden cross burning on his front lawn. This was a standard warning from the KKK. Its message: Stay in your place or expect trouble.

WONDER WHY?

Why do you think hate groups such as the KKK continue to exist today? What reasons do people give for joining such groups? What are their concerns? Do you think their concerns are legitimate?

"The problem of the twentieth century is the problem of the color line."

W.E.B. Du Bois (1868–1963),
Black educator and civil rights activist

If a Black person attempted to register to vote, KKK members might ride by their house at night and toss firebombs through their windows.

Across the South, illegal hangings, known as lynchings, took place with fearsome regularity. Sometimes, they took place in the dead of night. Sometimes, they took place in broad daylight, in public places such as parks or on the grounds of county courthouses.

Hooded members of the Ku Klux Klan turn out in support of Barry Goldwater's (1909–1998) presidential campaign in San Francisco, California, in 1964. In the decades after the Civil War, hate groups such as the KKK terrorized Black people throughout the South.

"Each time a man stands up for an ideal, or acts to improve the lot of others, or strikes out against injustice, he sends forth a tiny ripple of hope."

Robert F. Kennedy (1925–1968), attorney general of the United States and presidential candidate

BEING BLACK IN THE NORTH

Segregation and discrimination against Black people was an open story in the South. Were things better for African Americans in the North? In some respects, yes. In many other respects, however, their lives differed little from the lives of their Southern Black neighbors. Unfair housing practices meant that African Americans in Northern cities mostly lived in urban slums while whites lived in upscale apartments or moved out to the suburbs. Unfair employment practices meant that Black workers, regardless of their qualifications, were stuck in menial jobs. City police forces in the North were made up almost entirely of white officers. Their interactions with Black people were often as brutal as those of Southern police. Things had to change in the North as well as the South.

Either way, the murderers were rarely arrested. In fact, the mobs were usually assisted in their violence by the local police, who were themselves members of the KKK. How could equality and fairness possibly thrive in this kind of culture?

Starting a Movement

It must have seemed, at times, that nothing would ever change. But from the 1950s through the 1960s, African Americans and their allies challenged the old ways of segregation and discrimination. They demanded an end to injustice in American schools, in American courts, in American businesses, and in American politics.

CONNECT

Take a look at this brief history of the Civil Rights Movement, from Jim Crow to the election of Barack Obama (1961–) as president of the United States. What is the relationship between slavery and Jim Crow?

🔍 MoJo Civil Rights

To bring about these changes, Black Americans often risked everything—including their lives. It was common for civil rights activists to be physically attacked. Some were even murdered.

During the years of the Civil Rights Movement, the bravery of Black activists and their white supporters changed the course of American history. They narrowed the gap between the stated ideals of our country and the everyday reality of African American citizens.

Many people worked to change the racism that affected every aspect of life before the Civil Rights Movement, but a few stand out as leaders of their time. Thurgood Marshall, Fannie Lou Hamer, Martin Luther King Jr., Malcolm X, John Lewis, and Ella Baker all worked tirelessly to change the tide of societal habit and create a new, better world for future generations.

Medgar Evers's family meets with President John F. Kennedy, weeks after Evers was killed.

IN MEMORIAM

Medgar Evers (1925–1963) was a veteran of World War II, a college graduate, and a leader of the National Association for the Advancement of Colored People (NAACP) in Mississippi. His efforts to integrate Mississippi's public schools resulted in his death. On June 12, 1963, Evers was shot outside his home in Jackson, Mississippi, by Byron De La Beckwith (1920–2001), a member of a hate group called the White Citizens' Council. Evers was buried with full military honors at Arlington National Cemetery. What does his burial show about the way society viewed his death?

PROJECT

Civil Rights Issues Today

For as long as there has been a United States, there have been debates about civil rights. What civil rights issues are people concerned about today? Let's find out!

☮ **Conduct research on current civil rights issues.** Head to the library or use the internet to find out what people are fighting for or against. Are they the same issues people addressed during the Civil Rights Movement?

☮ **Use the following questions to guide your research.**

- What three or four civil rights issues seem to be the most urgent today?

- Does race continue to play a part in our concerns about civil rights? Why or why not?

- Does gender discrimination come up as a civil rights issue? If so, how and why?

- What other types of discrimination do people seem to be concerned about?

- Are any laws being proposed to expand civil rights to certain groups of people?

- Are any of these civil rights issues important to you? Why or why not?

☮ **Choose one issue that you feel is especially important and create a poster or other presentation that expresses your own beliefs about the issue.** Talk to classmates and family members to try to convince them that the issue is important. How does it feel to be a leader?

CONNECT

Environmental justice is becoming known as a civil rights issue. What is the connection between the two? What tool can climate change activists adopt from civil rights activists? Take a look at this video and see if you agree.

🔍 **Climate One civil environmental**

TEXT TO WORLD

Are people of different backgrounds treated differently from each other where you live? How?

This 1956 portrait of Thurgood Marshall by Betsy Graves Reyneau hangs in the National Portrait Gallery in Washington, DC.

CHAPTER ONE

THURGOOD
MARSHALL

FAST FACTS

BIRTH DATE:
July 2, 1908

PLACE OF BIRTH:
Baltimore, Maryland

AGE AT DEATH:
85

MAJOR ACCOMPLISHMENTS:

- Founder of the NAACP Legal Defense and Education Fund

- First African American U.S. solicitor general

- First African American Supreme Court justice

In 1946, Thurgood Marshall (1908–1993) was a well-respected lawyer who lived in an elite apartment building in New York City, New York. So, why was he racing around rural Tennessee, running from a bunch of angry white men who wanted to kill him?

Because he was Black, and he had just won "not guilty" verdicts for two Black men accused of trying to murder a white highway patrolman.

And in 1946 Tennessee, that was enough to get a Black man killed.

Roots

Thurgood Marshall was born into a Black neighborhood in Baltimore, Maryland. He was raised by parents who took pride in their accomplishments and looked forward to even better futures for their children.

His father, William Canfield Marshall, worked as a porter for the railroads and as a servant at an all-white country club. Those were two of the best jobs a Black man could have in the late nineteenth and early twentieth centuries. But he wanted better things for his sons, Thurgood and Thurgood's older brother, William.

WONDER WHY?

What are some of the jobs that people in your family hold? Do you ever think about joining that field? Does your family have any influence in your career goals?

" I never worked hard until I . . . met Charlie Houston. I saw this man's dedication . . . and I told myself, 'You either shape up or ship out.'"

Thurgood Marshall

CIVIL RIGHTS TIMELINE

1908 Thurgood Marshall is born in Baltimore, Maryland.

1933 Marshall graduates first in his class from Howard University School of Law.

1936 Marshall is hired as an attorney for the NAACP in New York City.

1940 Marshall successfully argues *Chambers v. Florida* before the U.S. Supreme Court. It overturns the convictions of four Black men falsely accused of killing a white man.

1942 Marshall successfully argues *Smith v. Allwright* to the Supreme Court, forcing Texas to allow Black people to vote in primary elections.

1948 Marshall successfully argues *Shelley v. Kraemer* before the Supreme Court. It opens the door for Black people to buy houses in all-white neighborhoods.

So, he introduced the boys to more interesting, lucrative careers. He entertained them with trips to local courthouses, where they watched prosecutors, defense attorneys, and judges in action.

Mr. Marshall also engaged his sons in debates about current events. Those family debates, Marshall said, "turned me into [a lawyer] . . . by making me prove every statement I made."

Marshall's mother, Norma Arica Williams, also shaped her sons' characters. A teacher with a master's degree in education, she ensured her sons received top-notch educations. When money was tight and college tuition was due, Mrs. Marshall once pawned her wedding rings to cover the expense.

Her sacrifices paid off. William became a doctor. Thurgood became a lawyer.

THE GREAT DEBATER

Debating was a way of life for Thurgood Marshall. He was always a star member of his schools' debate teams, but he also debated family members at home. He debated his teachers in the classroom. He debated friends at social gatherings. He was a great debater! And that skill paved the way for him to become one of the most successful lawyers of the twentieth century.

The School Prankster

Education was a serious matter in the Marshall household, but Marshall was not always a serious student. He was better known for playing practical jokes on people than for improving his mind. In college, his pranks got so out of hand he was suspended for bad behavior.

But all of that changed in 1929, when Marshall went to Howard University to study law. That was also the year he married his first wife, Vivian "Buster" Burey (1911–1955). From then on, Marshall worked harder than he ever had before. In 1933, he graduated at the top of his class with a law degree.

1950 Marshall successfully argues *Sweatt v. Painter* before the Supreme Court. It forces the University of Texas School of Law to enroll a Black student.

1954 Marshall wins *Brown v. Board of Education* in the Supreme Court. It opens the door to the integration of public schools.

1961 Marshall becomes a judge on the Second Circuit U.S. Court of Appeals, in New York City.

1965 Marshall becomes the first Black U.S. solicitor general.

1967 Marshall becomes the first Black associate justice of the U.S. Supreme Court.

1993 Marshall dies of heart failure in Bethesda, Maryland.

Joining the NAACP

Charles Hamilton Houston (1895–1950) was one of the most important figures in Thurgood Marshall's life. He was dean of Howard University School of Law when Marshall was a student. He was also the person who hired Marshall as a lawyer for the NAACP.

HISTORICALLY BLACK COLLEGES

Thurgood Marshall had wanted to attend law school at the University of Maryland, but that college accepted only white students. Marshall instead attended two historically Black colleges—Lincoln University in Pennsylvania and Howard University in Washington, DC. At Lincoln, he became friends with the legendary jazz singer Cab Calloway (1907–1994) and the award-winning poet Langston Hughes (1901–1967). What do you think are the advantages and disadvantages of historically Black colleges?

Langston Hughes, 1943

Credit: Gordon Parks

Jazz singer Cab Calloway, 1947

Credit: William Gottlieb

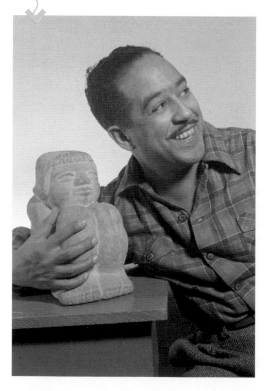

> **" A lawyer's either a social engineer or he's a parasite on society."**
>
> Charles Hamilton Houston

The NAACP was founded in 1909 to promote positive change for African Americans. By the 1930s, the group's main goal was to end legalized segregation. NAACP leadership believed that Black Americans would never advance until they had the same opportunities as white people.

But how could the NAACP force white society to open its schools, businesses, and neighborhoods to Black Americans?

CONNECT

Learn more about Charles Hamilton Houston and his fight for equal rights for African Americans using the law as a tool. Then, do some research on the anti-lynching law that passed in 2020. Why did it take so long?

🔍 **PBS Charles Houston Jim Crow**

The NAACP's answer to that question was to use the law. Starting in district courts and state courts, it would file lawsuits that argued segregationist laws were unconstitutional. Eventually, those lawsuits would wind up in the U.S. Supreme Court, where legal decisions could bring about significant social change.

Beginning in the 1930s, Houston served as special counsel to the NAACP. When Marshall graduated from Howard in 1933, he returned to Baltimore and opened his own law firm. But his business struggled financially. When Houston offered him a job at the NAACP, Marshall accepted the offer. In 1936, he and his wife, Buster, packed up and moved to New York City.

President John F. Kennedy meets with representatives from the NAACP in 1961, the year Kennedy appointed Thurgood Marshall to be a federal judge.

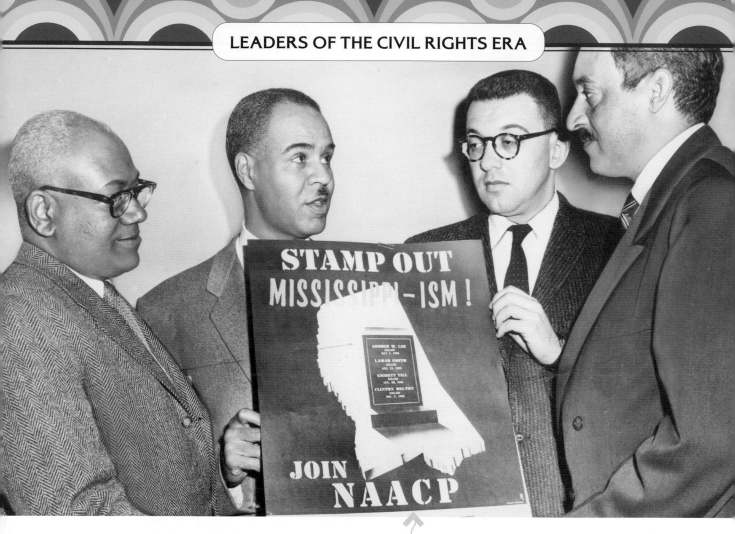

STAMP OUT MISSISSIPPI-ISM !

JOIN NAACP

Members of the NAACP hold up a Mississippi recruitment poster. From left to right they are Henry L. Moon, Roy Wilkins, Herbert Hill, and Thurgood Marshall.

Anytime the NAACP learned of another lynching, it hung this flag from its New York City offices.

A MAN WAS LYNCHED YESTERDAY

The Lower Courts

The NAACP pinned all of its hopes on getting cases heard before they made it to the Supreme Court. Why? If segregationist laws were unconstitutional, why did Southern judges in the lower courts uphold them in the first place?

The answer is simple. Many Southern judges were white supremacists. Their rulings supported white supremacy. We might think of judges as being impartial and unbiased tools meant to deliver rulings that are fair and equal, but that's not how it worked in the Jim Crow South.

CONNECT

Watch a series of mini biographies to learn more about Thurgood Marshall and his work for equal rights. Can you think of anyone today who is doing this same kind of work? What motivates them?

🔍 Thurgood Marshall videos

That's what made the Supreme Court so important. It was the one court where civil rights cases might be heard by more than one judge, all of whom were supposed to be unbiased.

🦅 FAMILY FACTS 🦅

Marshall married twice, first to Vivian "Buster" Burey in 1929 and then to Cecilia Suyat (1928–) in 1955, the year Buster died. He and Cecilia had two children—Thurgood Marshall Jr. (1956–) and John W. Marshall (1958–).

The U.S. Supreme Court in Washington, DC

Plessy v. Ferguson

Unfortunately, Supreme Court judges are not immune to bias and sometimes make decisions that uphold white supremacy. That was the case in a lawsuit known as *Plessy v. Ferguson*.

In 1892, Louisiana law required that railroad companies provide separate cars for Black people and white people. A Black man named Homer Plessy (1862–1925) challenged that law in court. He argued that the law denied him his civil rights, since the Fourteenth Amendment says all citizens must be treated equally.

THE LEGAL DEFENSE FUND

Changing an unconstitutional law is a long and costly process. It takes years for a case to work its way up from the lower courts to the Supreme Court. That's why, in 1940, Thurgood Marshall set up the NAACP Legal Defense Fund (LDF). This unit of the NAACP raised money to fund lawsuits for as many years as it might take to get a case heard before the Supreme Court.

A sign commonly found in restaurant windows under Jim Crow laws

WONDER WHY?

Do you think judges today are more or less biased than they were in the twentieth century? How might impartiality be measured? Why is this important?

Thurgood Marshall in 1967

Credit: Yoichi Robert

All the Southern lower courts ruled against Plessy. And in 1896, the Supreme Court ruled against him, too. Its ruling, however, included an important change: Making Black and white people ride in separate cars was okay, the judges said, *as long as the cars were of equal quality.*

CONNECT

Explore the case of *Dred Scott v. Sandford*, another Supreme Court case that changed the course of African American history. What are some of the repercussions of the Dred Scott case?

🔍 **Khan Academy Dred Scott v. Sandford**

The case *Plessy v. Ferguson* gave white supremacists a green light to maintain a segregated society. All they had to do was provide "separate but equal" facilities. Separate but equal bathrooms. Separate but equal drinking fountains. Separate but equal schools. Separate but equal everything!

But can equality really exist like that? No. Government officials who decide where city money is spent were overwhelmingly white. White schools, white facilities, and white services received more money than Black schools, facilities, and services. Separate, yes, but nowhere near equal.

To transform the Jim Crow South, the NAACP had to find a case that could overturn *Plessy v. Ferguson*. It was Thurgood Marshall's job to find that case, bring it to the Supreme Court, and convince the judges that *Plessy v. Ferguson* was unconstitutional.

WONDER WHY?

Does racial segregation still exist in American society? Why or why not? If so, how is it different?

But when Marshall brought the Brown's case to the Supreme Court, the outcome was very different. All nine judges ruled that segregated public schools were unconstitutional—even if the separate schools were equal in every way.

Brown v. Board of Education

Thurgood Marshall presented dozens of cases to the U.S. Supreme Court. But one stands out above all the others—*Brown v. Board of Education*.

The case itself was not unusual. A Black family by the name of Brown sued the school board of Topeka, Kansas, for refusing to enroll their daughter in an all-white public school. In all the lower Southern courts, the Brown family lost its case. The judges sided with the "separate but equal" standard set up by *Plessy v. Ferguson*.

The *Brown* case in 1954 accomplished what the NAACP had set out to do years before. It overturned *Plessy v. Ferguson*. It destroyed the idea that "separate but equal" was fair.

CONNECT

Learn how cases get to the Supreme Court. Why is it so hard for a case to be seen by this court?

🔍 **Vox Supreme Court**

Thurgood Marshall worked for the NAACP for 25 years. He argued 32 cases before the U.S. Supreme Court and won all but three of them. Marshall won so many civil rights cases, people referred to him as "Mr. Civil Rights."

Five years after the *Brown* ruling, white supremacists protest the integration of public schools in Arkansas.

Credit: John T. Bledsoe, Library of Congress

What the Brown Case Accomplished

You might imagine the *Brown* decision brought an immediate change in American society. That was not the case.

The *Brown* ruling stated that schools must be integrated with "all deliberate speed." That phrase left a lot to interpretation. White supremacists decided that meant they could integrate schools when they got around to it. And they never planned to get around to it.

WONDER WHY?

All but six of the 114 people appointed to the U.S. Supreme Court since it was established in 1789 have been white. How might this affect the laws in this United States? Do you think this ratio is fair?

President Lyndon Johnson meets with Thurgood Marshall in 1965.

On the surface, everything seemed the same, but in fact, everything was changing. The *Brown v. Board of Education* decision proved to African Americans that change was possible, and it became a starting point for the entire Civil Rights Movement. Inspired by their legal victory with *Brown* in 1954, African Americans from all walks of life started organizing for bigger changes to come.

With *Brown v. Board of Education*, Thurgood Marshall laid the groundwork for an American revolution.

THE MARSHALL PROJECT

Thurgood Marshall has inspired people to follow in his footsteps for generations. One such follower is Neil Barsky (1958–). Concerned about racial discrimination in the American criminal justice system, Barsky founded The Marshall Project in 2014. It is a nonprofit, online journalism platform that sheds light on the inequities Black people face in their dealings with police departments, courts, and correctional facilities. Why name his organization after Thurgood Marshall? In an open letter posted to The Marshall Project website, Barsky wrote that Marshall was an American hero. If Marshall were alive today, Barsky said, "I have no doubt that he would place criminal justice reform high among the urgent priorities of today's civil rights movement."

In 1961, President John F. Kennedy appointed Thurgood Marshall to be a federal judge.

After the NAACP

Thurgood Marshall left the NAACP in 1960, but his law career continued. In 1961, he became a federal judge. In 1965, he became the first Black U.S. solicitor general. And in 1967, he became a member of the U.S. Supreme Court.

He was the first Black man to wear the robes of an associate Supreme Court justice. He didn't take them off until he retired in 1991.

By the time Thurgood Marshall died at age 85, he was one of the most respected legal figures of his time. He was also one of the most revolutionary. Few lawyers have had a greater impact on the social fabric of America than Thurgood Marshall.

WONDER WHY?

In addition to being an intrepid thinker, Thurgood Marshall had a sense of humor. When he was a Supreme Court justice, he often greeted Chief Justice Warren E. Burger (1907–1995) with the line, "What's shaking, Chiefy Baby?" How can humor be useful in the struggle for equal rights?

PROJECT

Debate Current Events

Thurgood Marshall grew up debating current events. What current events might you debate today?

☮ **Watch a news broadcast, read a newspaper, or scroll through a newsfeed on your smartphone.** Then, prepare a written or visual presentation of a current event that interests you. Use the following questions to guide your work.

- What is your current event?
- Where is it taking place?
- Who does your event affect? Does it affect many people or just a few?

- Is this a recent issue or has it been in the news for a while?
- Why does this event interest you?
- What issues might you debate concerning this event?

☮ **Present your project to a class or group of friends or family.** Do any of them have a different opinion about your topic? What is their viewpoint? Engage in some debate with them and see if either of you can convince the other to change their mind.

What vocabulary words did you discover? Can you figure out the meanings of these words? Look in the glossary for help!

bias, debate, elite, defense attorney, impartial, pawn, porter, prosecutor, revolutionary, unbiased, and verdict

☮ **Consider how debating a topic makes you think more about it.** Even if you still have the same general opinion, do you know more about your current event than when you started debating it? Did you come up with more presentation points to include?

TEXT TO WORLD
How does the law affect your own day-to-day life?
How would your life change if certain laws changed?

PROJECT

Going to Court

Thurgood Marshall spent the first decades of his career as a lawyer representing clients in both criminal and civil courts. In this project, you're going to explore what it's like to prepare for your day in criminal court.

☮ **Read about a certain court case.** One day in July 2020, in Louisville, Kentucky, 100 peaceful protestors sat down on the front lawn of the attorney general of the state of Kentucky. They were protesting the fact that none of the Louisville police officers involved in the shooting of Breonna Taylor (1994–2020) three months earlier had been charged with murder. When the attorney general asked the protestors to get off his lawn, they refused to leave. Louisville police arrested all 100 protestors. Before the case of the "Lawn 100" goes to trial, see if you can find the answers to the following questions.

- Who was the attorney general of Kentucky in July 2020?
- What does a state attorney general do?
- Who are the defendants (the accused) in this case?
- Who are the prosecutors (the accusers) in this case?
- What law (or laws) can the prosecutors charge the defendants with breaking?
- Pretend that you are a prosecutor in this case. What three main points would you present to the jurors selected to determine the guilt or innocence of the Lawn 100.
- Pretend that you are defense attorney Thurgood Marshall. What three main points would you present to the jurors?

☮ **How is the information you found relative to the case?** Why is it critical to look at a crime from all sides? What role can the media play in ensuring fair trials for all?

Fannie Lou Hamer at the Democratic National Convention, Atlantic City, New Jersey, August 1964

Credit: Warren K. Leffler, *U.S. News & World Report* magazine collection

CHAPTER TWO

FANNIE LOU
HAMER

FAST FACTS

BIRTH DATE:
October 6, 1917

PLACE OF BIRTH:
Montgomery County,
Mississippi

AGE AT DEATH:
59

MAJOR ACCOMPLISHMENTS:

- Cofounder of the Mississippi Freedom Democratic Party

- Organizer of Mississippi's Freedom Summer

- Cofounder of the National Women's Political Caucus

Fannie Lou Hamer (1917–1977) grew up on a cotton plantation in Ruleville, Mississippi. She started picking cotton when she was 6, and when she was 13, she quit school so she could spend even more time at work picking cotton. It seemed as though she was meant to pick cotton for the rest of her life. What else could she do?

How about run for a seat in the U.S. Senate? In 1960, Hamer hadn't even realized she could vote. So, what happened to make her think she should run for the U.S. Senate in 1964?

What happened was the Civil Rights Movement. When Hamer started attending civil rights meetings, her life was transformed. She would not live and die in a cotton field.

Roots

Fannie Lou Hamer's home was in the Mississippi Delta, one of the richest cotton-growing areas in the United States. Technically, Fannie Lou, her parents, and her 19 brothers and sisters were free people. In reality, however, they were just one step removed from slavery.

CONNECT

Listen to an interview with Fannie Lou Hamer during her 1965 political campaign. What kinds of skills might she have that a political professional would not?

Fannie Lou Hamer interview 1965

The Hamers were Black sharecroppers and their lives were remarkably similar to those of their enslaved ancestors. They still lived on a plantation in ramshackle houses. They still worked for a white owner, doing the same backbreaking work. They still lived with the knowledge that they could be beaten, or even killed, by their white bosses and no one would suffer any consequences.

> " **I'm sick and tired of being sick and tired.**"
>
> Fannie Lou Hamer

The only difference between sharecropping and slavery was that the Black workers were paid. But, even then, their wages were very low and the plantation landowner charged them more money than they earned to cover the cost of rent and supplies.

CIVIL RIGHTS TIMELINE

1917 Fannie Lou Hamer is born in Montgomery County, Mississippi.

1930 Hamer leaves school at age 13 to work full time in the cotton fields.

1962 Hamer attempts to register to vote for the first time. She fails the voter literacy test.

1963 At her third attempt, Hamer passes the voter literacy test and becomes a registered voter.

1963 Hamer is jailed and beaten for trying to eat at a whites-only diner in Winona, Mississippi.

Day laborers pick cotton in Clarksdale, Mississippi, 1939.

Credit: Marion Post Wolcott

African Americans such as the Hamers lived in a cruel system of work, debt, and fear. It was a system that white supremacists were determined to keep, and a system that people such as Fannie Lou Hamer would dedicate their lives to upending.

CONNECT

Watch a short film from the perspective of people who knew Hamer. How might her upbringing have affected the work she did later as an adult?

🔍 **Hamer Stand Up MPB**

1964
Hamer runs for a seat in the U.S. Senate. She loses to Jamie Whitten (1910–1995), who had held the seat since 1941.

1964
Hamer plays a leading role in a Mississippi voter registration drive that becomes known as "Freedom Summer."

1969
Hamer forms the Freedom Farm Cooperative, designed to provide agricultural assistance to low-income African Americans.

1971
Hamer cofounds the National Women's Political Caucus.

1977
Hamer dies at age 59 due to complications brought on by high blood pressure and breast cancer.

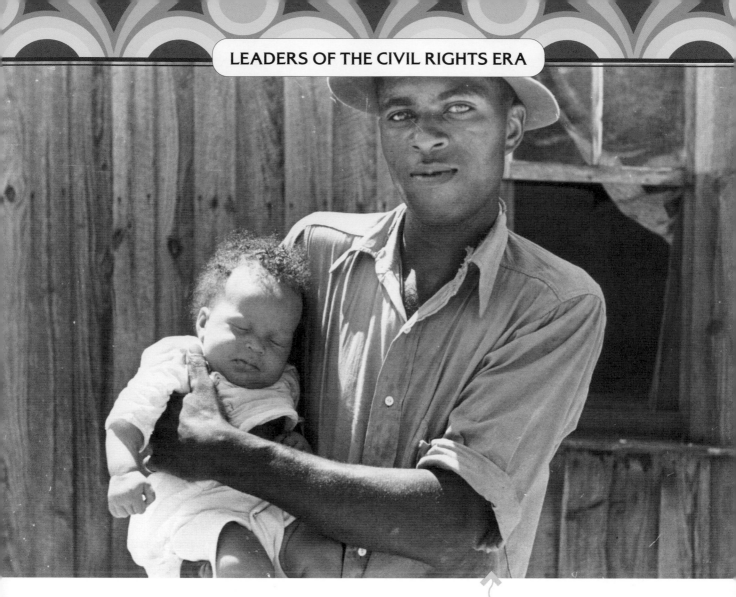

A tenant farmer in Mississippi, 1935

The Road to Activism

Fannie Lou Hamer can trace her entrance into the Civil Rights Movement back to one organization—the Regional Council of Negro Leadership (RCNL). Founded in 1951, the RCNL recruited local Black leaders to promote civil rights throughout Mississippi. It was at a rally of the RCNL in the 1950s that Hamer first truly understood that Black people could improve their lives simply by being able to vote.

WONDER WHY?

Do you think people in a democratic society have an obligation to vote? Why or why not?

Almost overnight, Hamer became one of those local Black leaders, working with the RCNL to inspire other people to take action.

Restrictive Voting Laws

By the time of the Civil Rights Movement, it was actually legal for men and women of all races to vote—thanks to the Fifteenth Amendment passed in 1870, which stated that voting rights could not be "denied or abridged by the United States or by any state on account of race, color, or previous condition of servitude."

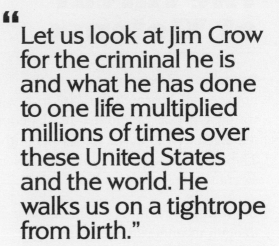

"Let us look at Jim Crow for the criminal he is and what he has done to one life multiplied millions of times over these United States and the world. He walks us on a tightrope from birth."

Rosa Parks (1913–2005), civil rights activist

So, why were Black people not voting in the Jim Crow South?

Black people didn't vote because white supremacists put a series of obstacles in their way. They charged poll taxes, for example—that is, they charged people to vote. Many African Americans simply couldn't afford the cost.

Another obstacle was voter literacy tests. In theory, these tests were supposed to keep poorly educated people from voting, which in itself was wrong. In practice, they kept only Black people from voting, because they were given only to Black people, and they were nearly impossible to pass.

These tests were never designed to measure intelligence. They were designed only to keep Black Americans from voting.

TAKE THE LITERACY TEST

The questions on the tests were of two sorts. They either asked very difficult questions or they asked questions that made no sense at all.

Here's an example of a question that was too hard to answer:

"If the Governor of Georgia dies, who succeeds him, and if both the Governor and the person who succeeds him die, who exercises the executive power?"

Now, here's an example of a nonsensical question:

"In the space below, write the word 'noise' backwards and place a dot over what would be its second letter should it have been written forward."

CONNECT

Could you pass a voter literacy test? You can try it at this website.

🔍 Thirteen voting literacy

The Threat of Violence

Poll taxes and voter literacy tests did not keep all African Americans from voting. One way or another, Black people managed to vote in the Jim Crow South. They even managed to win an occasional election.

But voting or running for office was a dangerous undertaking. When Black people tried to vote, they were often targeted by hate groups such as the KKK. Black people casting ballots risked being beaten. They risked being the victims of drive-by shootings. They risked having an enormous cross burned on their front lawns.

Small wonder so many didn't vote.

One Woman, One Vote

Hamer was 45 years old when she decided it was time she registered to vote. On August 31, 1962, she and 18 other Black activists headed to Indianola, Mississippi, to become registered voters.

As expected, a white clerk presented Hamer with a voter literacy test. Stumped by a question about "de facto" laws, Hamer failed the test. "I knowed [sic] as much about 'facto' law as a horse knows about Christmas day," Hamer said.

FAMILY FACTS

Fannie Lou Hamer was born Fannie Lou Townsend. She changed her name when she married Perry "Pap" Hamer (1912–1992), a tractor driver on the Marlow Plantation. Fannie Lou and Pap had no biological children, but they adopted two daughters.

Future voters at a voter registration drive sometime in the 1960s

Credit: Kheel Center, Cornell University Library (CC BY 2.0)

" [W]hat was the point of being scared? The only thing they could do was kill me, and it kinda seemed like they'd been trying to do that a little bit at a time since I could remember."

Fannie Lou Hamer

Hamer's attempt to register was also met with violence. On September 10, the house Hamer was staying in was shot at 16 times by a drive-by shooter. Miraculously, no one was injured.

Despite the threats on her life, Hamer returned to Indianola on December 4, 1962. She failed the voter literacy test again. But before she left, Hamer told the clerk, "You'll see me every 30 days till I pass."

Hamer was true to her word. On January 10, 1963, she returned to Indianola yet again. This time, she passed the voter literacy test and became a registered voter in the state of Mississippi.

Failing the voter literacy test, however, was only the start of Hamer's problems. When she returned home, the owner of the Marlow Plantation fired Hamer from her job and ordered her off his property—because she had tried to register to vote.

WONDER WHY?

Fannie Lou Hamer risked her life for the right to vote. How important is the right to vote to you?

The Price She Paid

Registering to vote had nearly cost Fannie Lou Hamer her life. But it would not be the last time her work in the Civil Rights Movement put her in harm's way. Perhaps knowing the danger that African Americans faced when they stood up for equal rights galvanized her to work even harder.

In June 1963, Hamer was among a group of Black activists who tried to eat at a whites-only diner in Winona, Mississippi. Some of the group, including Hamer, were arrested, taken to jail, and severely beaten.

> " **When I liberate myself, I liberate others. If you don't speak out, ain't nobody going to speak out for you.**"
>
> Fannie Lou Hamer

The assault nearly killed Hamer. It left her with injuries that caused her pain for the rest of her life and might have contributed to her early death at age 59.

Freedom Summer

In 1962, less than 7 percent of Mississippi's eligible Black voters were registered to vote. That's why, in 1964, civil rights groups organized a massive Black voter registration drive in Mississippi. Their goal was to register as many Black voters in Mississippi as they could.

Credit: dignidadrebelde (CC BY 2.0)

The organizers, including Hamer, leaned on the talent of local Black activists to lead the campaign. They also sought assistance beyond Mississippi. In particular, they reached out to white students from Northern colleges.

Hamer believed that America's race problems would never be solved until Black people and white people worked together. As a result, she took a leading role in recruiting and training out-of-state white students to help in her home state—more than 700 mostly white young people traveled south to help register Black voters.

The 1964 campaign in Mississippi became known as "Freedom Summer."

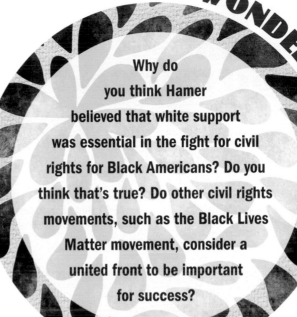

WONDER WHY?

Why do you think Hamer believed that white support was essential in the fight for civil rights for Black Americans? Do you think that's true? Do other civil rights movements, such as the Black Lives Matter movement, consider a united front to be important for success?

Almost from the start, it was met with violent resistance. In just 10 weeks, more than 1,000 Freedom Summer volunteers were arrested, dozens were beaten, 37 Black churches and 30 Black homes or businesses were bombed or burned, and four civil rights workers were killed.

Despite this reign of terror, Freedom Summer activists succeeded in registering 1,000 new Black voters in Mississippi. Perhaps more importantly, they proved that no amount of resistance would keep them from pushing ahead with their goal of ensuring that Black Americans were allowed to vote.

THIS LITTLE LIGHT

Fannie Lou Hamer grew up attending churches where singing was an important part of religious services. She became a powerful gospel singer, and her singing became an important part of her work in the Civil Rights Movement. In moments of danger, her singing calmed frayed nerves. If fellow activists were discouraged, her singing renewed their hope. In moments of triumph, her singing was a celebration. Hamer's signature song was the gospel tune "This Little Light of Mine." The simple refrain, "This little light of mine, I'm gonna let it shine," summed up her irrepressible spirit. Are there other situations where music plays an important role? How does singing as a group affect us? How does it make us feel? Have any specific songs risen up from the more recent Black Lives Matter movement?

CONNECT

Listen to Fannie Lou Hamer sing "This Little Light of Mine."

🔍 Hamer little light

Mississippi Freedom Democratic Party

The Freedom Summer campaign did not register as many Black voters as the activists had hoped for. But Hamer did not let that disappointment keep her from forging ahead.

Supporters of the Mississippi Freedom Democratic Party at the 1964 Democratic National Convention, New Jersey

Credit: Warren K. Leffler

Her next target was the Democratic Party of Mississippi. A political party is supposed to be open to all people. But the Democratic Party in Mississippi excluded Black people. During the 1960s, more Black people than white people lived in Mississippi. Yet they had zero representation in the Democratic Party. How could this be considered equal?

To challenge that racist system, Hamer and others created a new political party—the Mississippi Freedom Democratic Party (MFDP). Membership in the MFDP was open to everyone—and thousands joined.

A Black Woman Speaks

In August 1964, Hamer and others from the MFDP attended the national convention of the Democratic Party in Atlantic City, New Jersey. Their goal was to push out the whites-only Democratic Party and replace it with the MFPD.

When Fannie Lou Hamer was called to testify to the Credential Committee, she spoke of the violence that had met her and other Black people when they tried to register to vote.

Her testimony was considered so disturbing and disruptive that the White House called a press conference in the middle of it to prevent it from airing on television—remember, this was in the days before YouTube! Viewers had hardly any choice in what they could watch on television. However, the story of her testimony only grew because politicians tried to stifle it.

CONNECT

You can listen to parts of her speech at this website. Why do you think people were so uncomfortable about what she was saying? What might it make them consider?

🔍 American Experience Fannie Hamer

Hamer's speech struck a chord with people throughout the country. "Is this America," she asked, "the land of the free and the home of the brave?"

Unfortunately, the MFDP did not replace the all-white Democratic Party from Mississippi. But that doesn't mean the activists' efforts failed. The Democratic Party *did* change. Four years later, in 1968, the Democratic Party required equal racial representation among all state delegations. In 1972, Hamer herself was elected as a national party delegate.

Even more significant was passage in 1965 of the Voting Rights Act. This law prohibited racial discrimination in voting—the very thing Hamer had risked her life to achieve.

[1971]

Elect
INFORMED

SINCERE

CAPABLE

MRS.
Fannie Lou HAMER

STATE SENATOR
District 11 — Post No. 2
BOLIVAR AND SUNFLOWER COUNTIES
NOVEMBER 2, 1971

A political poster from 1971

WONDER WHY?

Why might creating a new political party further the goal of equal representation faster than working from within existing parties?

Civil rights activist Andrew Young spoke at Fannie Lou Hamer's funeral.

WONDER WHY?

How has the fight for civil rights been built on the activism of the past? How do we see this working today with the Black Lives Matter movement? How is that struggle based on work that was done decades ago?

The Legend of Fannie Lou

When Fannie Lou Hamer was a little girl picking cotton, she never imagined that songs, plays, and movies would be written about her life. She didn't foresee schools and post offices being named after her. She had no idea she would be elected into the National Women's Hall of Fame.

Yet all those things happened. They happened because Hamer found her purpose in the Civil Rights Movement, and because she had the courage to lead her people.

Hamer died young, at age 59, due to complications brought on by high blood pressure and breast cancer. Among the 1,500 people who attended her funeral was Andrew Young (1932–), a Black activist and the future mayor of Atlanta, Georgia. Young summed up Hamer's importance: "None of us would be where we are now," he said, "had she not been there then."

Word Power!

What vocabulary words did you discover? Can you figure out the meanings of these words? Look in the glossary for help!

activism, de facto, eligible, irrepressible, obligation, poll tax, prohibit, representative, and voter literacy test

" You don't run away from problems. You just face them."

Fannie Lou Hamer

WOMEN'S RIGHTS

Fannie Lou Hamer demanded equal rights for everybody, including women. She was a member of the National Council of Negro Women and cofounder of the National Women's Political Caucus (NWPC). Both organizations trained women to take leading roles in their communities. Founding members of the NWPC included some of the most important leaders in the women's rights movement of the twentieth century. They included Shirley Chisholm (1924–2005), the first Black woman elected to the U.S. House of Representatives; Bella Abzug (1920–1998), a U.S. representative from New York City; and Gloria Steinem (1934–), cofounder of *Ms.* magazine, an influential feminist publication.

PROJECT

Positive Change for Women

The voting rights efforts of the Civil Rights Movement did not mark the first time in American history that citizens demanded access to the ballot. That distinction goes to the women's suffrage movement of the nineteenth and twentieth centuries. It was a decades-long struggle that ended in 1920 with passage of the Nineteenth Amendment to the Constitution.

☮ **Visit the library or use the internet to research the women's suffrage movement.** The following questions can help you get started.

· Why was the right to vote initially limited to landowners? How did that prevent most women from voting?

· How did the movement to abolish slavery influence women's thinking about voting rights?

· What skills did women learn in their efforts to end slavery?

· When slavery was abolished, why did women believe they might be given the right to vote?

· What were some of the strategies that suffrage activists used to promote their cause?

CONNECT

Watch a short documentary about the women's suffrage movement. How was it connected to the abolitionist movement?

🔍 **Annenbergclassroom women's right vote**

· Why did it take so long for the Nineteenth Amendment to become law?

☮ **Compare and contrast women's struggle to gain the right to vote with the Civil Rights Movement.** How might the Civil Rights Movement have been different if women hadn't organized earlier in the century? What would life be like now for women had they never gained the vote?

TEXT TO WORLD — Why are voting rights so important? Are any groups discouraged or prevented from voting today?

PROJECT

Music of the Movement

Fannie Lou Hamer's singing was an important element of the Civil Rights Movement, as was the music of many other artists.

⚛ **Three of the most popular civil rights songs are listed here.** Listen to each one; then, discuss the following questions among your friends or family.

- In what ways are the songs similar and different?
- How does each song make you feel?
- If you knew you were going to face an angry mob at a protest, which song would you most like to hear? Why?

☮ **Write the lyrics or a poem to create your own protest song!** What images do you think will make other people consider your viewpoint?

"We Shall Overcome," performed by The Morehouse College Glee Club

🔎 **We Shall Overcome**

"Blowin' in the Wind," performed by Peter, Paul, and Mary

🔎 **Blowin' in the Wind**

"Freedom Highway," performed by The Staple Singers

🔎 **Freedom Highway**

Folk singers Joan Baez and Bob Dylan sing at the March on Washington in 1964.

The only known photograph of Martin
Luther King Jr. and Malcolm X, 1964.

CHAPTER THREE

MARTIN
LUTHER KING JR. AND
MALCOLM X

Two figures of the Civil Rights Movement—Martin Luther King Jr. and Malcolm X—represented two different sides of Black America. Martin Luther King Jr. stood for desegregation and nonviolence. Malcolm X stood for separation and self-defense.

FASTFACTS

MARTIN LUTHER KING JR.

BIRTH DATE:
January 15, 1929

PLACE OF BIRTH:
Atlanta, Georgia

AGE AT DEATH:
39

MAJOR ACCOMPLISHMENTS:

- Leader of the 1955 Montgomery, Alabama, bus boycott

- President of the Southern Christian Leadership Conference

- Winner of the Nobel Peace Prize in 1964

MALCOLM X

BIRTH DATE:
May 19, 1925

PLACE OF BIRTH:
Omaha, Nebraska

AGE AT DEATH:
39

MAJOR ACCOMPLISHMENTS:

- Leading figure of the Black Nationalist Movement

- Influential Muslim minister of the Nation of Islam

- Founder of Muslim Mosque Inc. and the Organization of Afro-American Unity

During the Civil Rights Era, most Black Americans agreed that changes needed to be made in American society. However, they did not always agree on what those changes ought to be or how to bring them about.

> "We are determined to gain our rightful place in God's world. We are determined to be men. We are determined to be people."
>
> Martin Luther King Jr.

Some activists wanted to create a society where Black and white people lived and worked together. Others wanted Black people and white people to live totally apart.

Many vowed that when violence was done to them, they would not retaliate with violence of their own. Others said they should defend themselves. Who was right?

He was also the leader of a civil rights protest that was growing bigger by the day. Fed up with segregated city buses, the 50,000 Black residents of Montgomery were refusing to ride the buses until the company dropped its racist policies.

CONNECT

Listen to Martin Luther King Jr. respond to a comment from Malcolm X. How do you think their two ideologies fit together or don't fit together?

🔍 uzitone King Malcolm X

Eyes Open to Nonviolence

In the final days of 1955, Martin Luther King Jr. was a frightened young man. He was the new minister at the Dexter Avenue Baptist Church in Montgomery, Alabama.

CIVIL RIGHTS TIMELINE

1925 Malcolm X is born in Omaha, Nebraska.

1929 Martin Luther King Jr. is born in Atlanta, Georgia.

1944 King enrolls at Morehouse College in Atlanta, Georgia.

1946 Malcolm is sentenced to prison on burglary charges.

1952 Released from prison, Malcolm becomes a minister with the Nation of Islam.

1954 King becomes minister of the Dexter Avenue Baptist Church in Montgomery, Alabama.

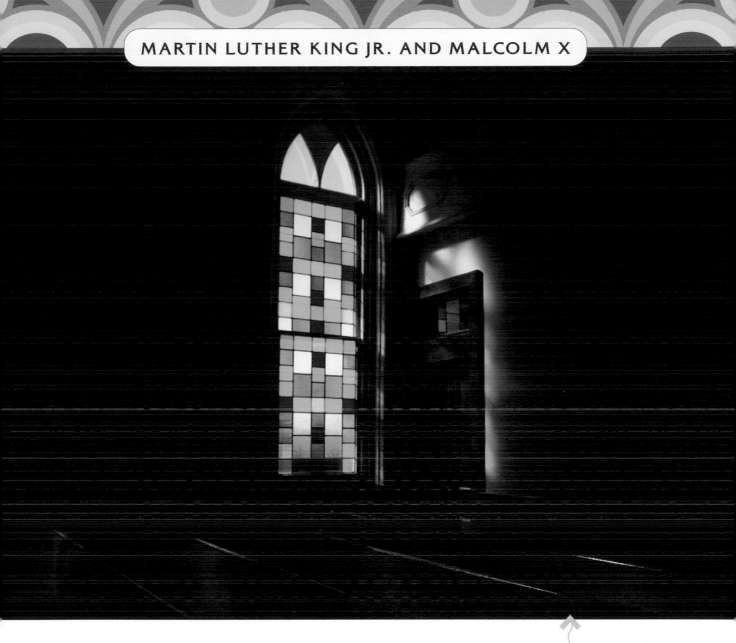

Dr. King's church

White supremacists in Montgomery were furious. Hoping to bring the boycott to a quick end, they threatened the boycott's leader, Dr. King. He answered his telephone one night and heard someone promising to "blow your brains out and blow up your house."

1955	1957	1963	1964	1965	1965	1968
King helps guide the Montgomery bus boycott to success.	Malcolm leads 4,000 Black people through a peaceful demonstration against police brutality in Harlem, New York.	King delivers his famous "I Have a Dream" speech to 250,000 at the March on Washington.	Malcolm delivers his famous "The Ballot or the Bullet" speech at a Methodist church in Cleveland, Ohio.	Members of the Nation of Islam assassinate Malcolm X at the Audubon Ballroom in New York City.	King leads a march for voting rights from Selma to Montgomery, Alabama.	James Earl Ray assassinates King at the Lorraine Motel in Memphis, Tennessee.

Dr. King had armed himself with a handgun. But he was still afraid. Alone in his kitchen, King prayed for God to help him. He said, years later, that Jesus spoke to him. He told King to "stand up for righteousness . . . stand up for the truth."

From that moment on, King committed himself to the use of nonviolent resistance to racism. He got rid of his gun and prepared to lead his people in peaceful protest.

Roots

Martin Luther King Jr. was born and raised in Atlanta, Georgia, where his life revolved around the Ebenezer Baptist Church. His mother, Alberta Williams King (1904–1974), played the church organ and sang in the choir. His father, the Reverend Martin Luther King Sr. (1899–1984), was the church's minister and an early activist in the Civil Rights Movement.

WONDER WHY?

How did King's faith support his activism? How do you think people reacted to his role as minister?

WAS KING A DOCTOR?

Morehouse College, Atlanta, Georgia

Credit: giggle (CC BY 2.0)

We often refer to Martin Luther King Jr. as Dr. King, but not because he was a doctor who treated people for illnesses. King was called "doctor" because he earned a doctoral degree, or a PhD, which stands for "doctor of philosophy." Anyone who receives a doctoral degree earns the right to be addressed as "Dr."

Martin Luther King Jr. earned a degree in sociology from Morehouse College in Atlanta, Georgia, and a doctoral degree from the Boston University School of Theology in Boston, Massachusetts.

It was near Atlanta where King also experienced one of the greatest humiliations of his life. He was a teenager riding an interstate bus with a teacher on a school field trip when the bus driver ordered King and his teacher to give their seats to white passengers. Enraged, King stood for the entire 90-mile trip. He later said the incident made him "hate every white person."

So, what caused Dr. King to turn away from his hatred of white people and embrace a philosophy of nonviolent protest?

Martin Luther King Jr. in 1964

Credit: Dick DeMarsico, *New York World-Telegram & Sun* staff photographer

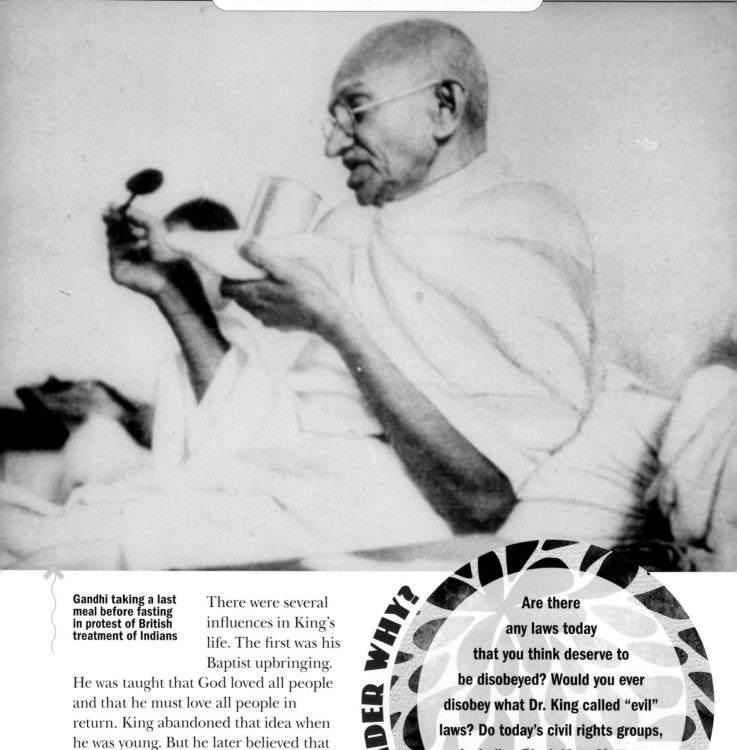

Gandhi taking a last meal before fasting in protest of British treatment of Indians

There were several influences in King's life. The first was his Baptist upbringing. He was taught that God loved all people and that he must love all people in return. King abandoned that idea when he was young. But he later believed that God's love really could change even the most hardened racists.

WONDER WHY?

Are there any laws today that you think deserve to be disobeyed? Would you ever disobey what Dr. King called "evil" laws? Do today's civil rights groups, including Black Lives Matter, practice nonviolent protest?

King was also inspired by the American author Henry David Thoreau (1817–1862). His book, *On Civil Disobedience,* published in 1849, argued that people had a moral duty to disobey unjust laws. Thoreau used slavery as an example. If it was wrong to own another human being, then it was right to disobey laws that upheld slavery.

Another role model was Mahatma Gandhi (1869–1948). Gandhi helped India gain its freedom from British rule by organizing nonviolent protests that involved Indians peacefully disobeying British laws. British officers beat, jailed, and even killed the Indian protestors. But the peaceful protests worked. In 1947, Great Britain gave up its control over India.

> **"We will meet the forces of hate with the power of love . . . . We will match your capacity to inflict suffering with our capacity to endure suffering."**
>
> Martin Luther King Jr.

The First Test

In 1955, Martin Luther King Jr. had no idea he was about to become the most recognized civil rights leader of his time.

But that is exactly what happened after Rosa Parks (1913–2005) refused to move to the back of the bus behind white passengers on a Montgomery city bus. A Black activist and a member of the NAACP, Parks knew she would be arrested and taken to jail that Thursday afternoon. Her refusal to give up her seat was a deliberate tactic to expose racism in Montgomery.

ROSA PARKS

It was not by accident that Rosa Parks refused to give up her bus seat to a white passenger in Montgomery, Alabama. A seamstress at local department store, Parks was also an officer in the Montgomery NAACP, and she had received training in nonviolent protest at the Highlander Folk School in Tennessee. Parks's refusal to comply with a racist law was the first step in a planned action organized by the NAACP. Members chose Parks to set the plan in motion because she possessed the skills and the courage to see things through to the end.

CONNECT

Can someone who has never experienced or witnessed racism learn about it? During the 1960s, a teacher named Jane Elliot developed a method to do this based on eye color. Read an article and watch a video about her teachings at this website.

🔍 **People Jane Elliot**

By Monday morning, local Black leaders had organized a boycott of the city's buses. By Monday afternoon, King was elected to lead the boycott as head of the new Montgomery Improvement Association (MIA). And Monday night, he delivered an inspiring speech to 4,000 people at one of the largest Black churches in the city.

CONNECT

Read Dr. King's first Montgomery bus boycott speech. How do public speeches help a social movement? Have you heard any speeches related to more recent protests such as the Black Lives Matter movement that were impressive to you?

🔍 blackpast the Montgomery bus boycott

When the boycott ended nearly a year later, the Montgomery buses were desegregated. The Black population of Montgomery had proved that nonviolent protests could result in real change. The Civil Rights Movement had begun. And King was famous.

Rosa Parks being fingerprinted after her arrest

Beyond the Bus Boycott

Encouraged by their success in Montgomery, Black activists formed a new group to keep the momentum going. They called themselves the Southern Christian Leadership Conference, or SCLC. Dr. King was its first president.

Under King's direction, the SCLC pressed for racial justice by constantly staging peaceful, nonviolent protests.

> " We will not hate you, but we will not obey your evil laws."
>
> Martin Luther King Jr.

For several weeks during the spring of 1963, for example, the SCLC organized a series of protests in Birmingham, Alabama. Black people wanted to bring their concerns about racial segregation to the mayor, Albert Boutwell (1904–1978). They gathered at the 16th Street Baptist Church and, 50 people at a time, they walked from the church to the town hall. But instead of meeting with the protestors, Mayor Boutwell refused to talk to them.

Bomb-damaged trailers at the Gaston Motel, Birmingham, Alabama, 1963

Credit: Marion S. Trikosko, *U.S. News & World Report* magazine collection

Worse still were the actions of Police Chief Eugene "Bull" Connor (1897–1973) and his all-white police force. Police beat Black protestors with nightsticks, attacked them with police dogs, and sprayed them with fire hoses. The streams of water were so powerful they pushed small children down the sidewalk.

These violent acts were reported in newspapers, magazines, and on television news broadcasts around the country. Many people, seeing images of raw racial hatred for the first time, were shocked. They echoed the words of Fannie Lou Hamer. "Is this America?" they asked in disbelief.

There was still a long way to go, however, and much to do in the name of equality.

WONDER WHY?

Why might people react more to images of violence than to written or verbal reports of violence? Does that hold true today?

The March on Washington

Violent incidents such as those in Birmingham forced Americans to confront the race problems in their country. If they had been unaware of racial injustice before, they were certainly aware of it now.

> " And one of the problems is there is too much high-octane hypocrisy in America. There is a lot of noble talk about brotherhood and then some Americans drop the brother and keep the hood."
>
> Walter Reuther (1907 – 1970), president of United Auto Workers and civil rights activist, speaking at the March on Washington

By the summer of 1963, the time seemed ripe for a nationwide demonstration. Six civil rights organizations organized a rally in the nation's capital. Called the March on Washington for Jobs and Freedom, the rally took place on August 28, 1963. An estimated 250,000 people came from across the country to listen to speeches by the most important civil rights leaders of the day.

The March on Washington, 1963

Credit: From the *U.S. News & World Report* magazine collection at the Library of Congress

The highlight of the rally came when Dr. King addressed the crowd in front of the Lincoln Memorial. Dr. King described his dream of a day when all people would be treated as equals. Known now as the "I Have a Dream" speech, King's words inspired countless people.

CONNECT

Listen to King's speech at the March on Washington. Do his words still apply to racial equality today? How are things different? How are they the same?

🔍 King I Have a Dream

The March on Washington did not end racism in the United States. But the presence of more than 200,000 Black people standing up for their own rights sent a clear message to the country.

Black Americans were not going to accept racial injustice any longer. The country was going to have to change.

The Commitment to Nonviolence

Dr. King believed that love and nonviolence could change the attitudes of white supremacists. But refraining from violence was never easy. When white people attacked Black activists, it was only natural for them to want to strike back. King worried that he might not be able to hold back the violence.

Such was the case in St. Augustine, Florida, in 1964, when a group of Black SCLC protestors tried to walk peacefully into a white section of town. They were set upon by a mob of 800 angry white supremacists. Attacking the protestors with tire irons, baseball bats, logging chains, and pool sticks, the angry mob chased the peaceful protesters back into the Black section of town.

There, an injured woman cried out in the streets: "To hell with this nonviolence!" Black men armed themselves with guns. They prepared to defend themselves and their families against white violence.

King called his followers into a church and further violence was avoided. But that same night, King admitted his fears to the journalist Marshall Frady (1940–2004). "What are we doing to these people?" he said. "It can't go on like this. . . . It just can't go on like this."

 FAMILY FACTS

King married Coretta Scott (1927–2006) in 1953. They had four children—Yolanda King (1955–2007), Martin Luther King III (1957–), Dexter Scott King (1961–), and Bernice King (1963–).

The old slave market in St. Augustine, Florida, was the site of white supremacist violence in 1964.

The Assassination

But the violence did continue. From 1954 to 1968, at least 41 civil rights activists were killed as a result of their involvement with the movement. Thousands more were injured.

Dr. King himself lived under a constant threat of death. His house had been firebombed during the Montgomery bus boycott, and ever since, white supremacists had vowed to kill him.

For 13 years, Dr. King lived with the expectation that he would be murdered. His fears were finally realized in Memphis, Tennessee. On April 4, 1968, he was in Memphis to support Black sanitation workers who were demanding equal pay for equal work. At 6 p.m., King stepped onto the balcony of his room at the Lorraine Motel, and James Earl Ray (1928–1998) shot him from across the street. King died an hour later at a local hospital.

WONDER WHY?

What would have happened if Black protestors had resorted to using violence in St. Augustine? Do you think that would have helped or hurt the Civil Rights Movement?

Assassination's Aftermath

The murder of Dr. King sent shock waves through Black communities across the United States. People grieved the death of a beloved leader, and in many places, that grief expressed itself as civil unrest.

Uprisings erupted in more than 100 cities, including Washington, DC; Chicago, Illinois; Baltimore, Maryland; and Detroit, Michigan. Stores were looted, buildings and cars were set on fire, and protestors clashed with law enforcement.

More than 14,000 people were arrested. Thousands were injured. An estimated 40 people died.

Malcolm X and the Case for Black Nationalism

While Martin Luther King Jr. spoke of integration and nonviolence, Malcolm X poured his energy into encouraging Black Americans to separate completely from white society. And if white supremacists attacked them, he encouraged people to defend themselves.

Malcolm X in 1964

BLACK SELF-DEFENSE

In Oakland, California, in 1966, police brutality against Black residents prompted college students Bobby Seale (1936–) and Huey Newton (1942–1989) to take action. They formed the Black Panther Party for Self-Defense. Black Panther members armed themselves with guns and organized themselves into citizen patrols to safeguard Oakland's Black residents from police misconduct. As the organization evolved, the Black Panthers supported the Black community in other ways as well. For example, they provided free breakfast to children and opened community health clinics.

Black anger and frustration were things he knew only too well. He tapped into those feelings to become the unrivaled spokesperson for the idea of Black nationalism.

Garvey imagined a time when Black Americans owned their own businesses, ran their own schools, founded their own hospitals, and formed their own banks. They would do everything for themselves. They would owe nothing to white America.

Roots

Malcolm X was born Malcolm Little, the fourth of seven children born to Earl Little and Louise Little (1897–1991). Both of Malcolm X's parents were heavily involved in a Black separatist organization known as the Universal Negro Improvement Association (UNIA). Formed by Marcus Garvey (1887–1940) in 1914, the UNIA encouraged all people of African descent to free themselves from white society.

> " **Our success . . . is based upon the protection of a nation founded by ourselves. And the nation can be nowhere else but in Africa.**"
>
> **Marcus Garvey**

Garvey even hoped that eventually, Black Americans would form their own nation in their ancestral home of Africa.

The Malcolm X Memorial Foundation visitor center in Omaha, Nebraska

White Violence

Malcolm X's parents' involvement with the UNIA came at a cost. Their activism drew the attention of a hate group known as the Black Legion, which terrorized Malcolm X's family.

In 1929, the Littles were living in Lansing, Michigan, when their home burned to the ground. No one could say for sure what started the blaze, but Malcolm X's parents had no doubt it had been set by white supremacists.

A couple of years later, Malcolm X's father died in a highly suspicious and violent incident. He went out one evening in 1931 to run errands and never returned home. He was found with his head bashed in and his body cut nearly in half on the rails of a street car track. The police ruled the death an accident. But many believed Earl Little had been murdered by the Black Legion.

> " What I want to know is how the white man, with the blood of Black people dripping off his fingers, can . . . [ask] Black people, 'Do they hate him?' That takes a lot of nerve."
>
> Malcolm X

The End of Formal Education

By the time he was 6 years old, Malcolm X had realized that death was the price his own father paid for trying to improve his station in life. In school, Malcolm X learned that he shouldn't even try to improve his own life.

Malcolm X had a sharp mind and an engaging personality. When he was in junior high school, he imagined putting those skills to use by becoming a lawyer. A white teacher, however, told Malcolm X such goals were unrealistic for a Black boy. He should set his sights lower.

After that incident, Malcolm X lost interest in educating himself. He dropped out of school and supported himself with the low-paying jobs that were available to Black men at that time.

Marcus Garvey, shown here in 1924, founded the United Negro Improvement Association.

Credit: From the George Grantham Bain Collection

Malcolm X also became involved in the underground, illegal economy of drug dealing and burglary. Eventually, his illegal activities caught up with him. In 1945, he was arrested for burglary in Boston, Massachusetts. Found guilty at trial, he was sentenced to 8 to 10 years in prison.

Elijah Muhammad, shown here speaking in 1964, was the leader of the Nation of Islam during Malcolm X's lifetime.

Becoming Malcolm X

Malcolm Little stayed in prison for six years, from 1946 to 1952, and it was there that he reinvented himself as Malcolm X.

Malcolm X's brothers and sisters visited him in prison. They told him about a Black man named Elijah Muhammad (1897–1975) and the religious organization he represented, the Nation of Islam. The Nation of Islam was a branch of Islam that accepted only Black people into its fold. Its spiritual leader was Elijah Muhammad.

Like Marcus Garvey before him, Elijah Muhammad taught that Black people would never reach their full potential until they freed themselves from white society. In his view, white people were responsible for slavery, Jim Crow segregation, and the murder of Black people. Followers of the Nation of Islam could have nothing to do with them.

Minister Malcolm X

At first, Malcolm X resisted the teachings of Elijah Muhammad. But when he considered the cruel treatment that Black people had suffered for hundreds of years, he eventually accepted the theory that white people were, in fact, devils. Soon, Malcolm X joined the Nation of Islam. He became one of Elijah Muhammad's most devoted followers.

Malcolm X served as a Nation of Islam minister at Temple No. 7, in Harlem until he left the group in 1964. The temple is now known as Malcolm Shabazz Mosque.

CONNECT

Listen to Malcolm X deliver a fiery speech in Los Angeles, California, in 1962. Could his words apply to relations between Black people and police today? Why do you think society hasn't come further in terms of racial equality?

🔍 Malcolm X Smithsonian police brutality

Released from prison in 1952, Malcolm X went to work as a minister for the Nation of Islam. He was spectacularly effective at bringing large numbers of new members into the Nation of Islam. Wherever Malcolm went—from Boston to Detroit, Philadelphia to Harlem— membership in the Nation of Islam dramatically increased.

Within just a couple of years, Malcolm X was the most recognized representative of the Nation of Islam. He was invited to speak at colleges, universities, and civic organizations. He was interviewed by print and broadcast journalists. Documentaries were made about him. Books were written about him.

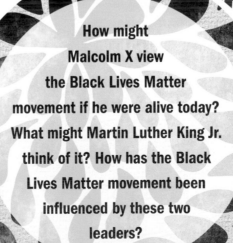

WONDER WHY?

How might Malcolm X view the Black Lives Matter movement if he were alive today? What might Martin Luther King Jr. think of it? How has the Black Lives Matter movement been influenced by these two leaders?

The Black Nationalist Message

Many people—especially white people—did not like the message that Malcolm X broadcast to the world. They didn't like hearing that Black people were violently oppressed. They didn't like hearing that white people could not be trusted. They didn't like hearing the March on Washington called the "Farce on Washington." They didn't like Black people being told to arm themselves and protect their families from white supremacist attacks.

For many Black Americans, however, Malcolm X's words rang true. Black people, in fact, *were* violently oppressed. Victories in the Supreme Court and mass demonstrations changed very little. Schools and neighborhoods were still segregated. High-paying jobs were still hard to find.

> "You don't have a revolution in which you love your enemy . . . . Revolutions overturn systems. Revolutions destroy systems."
>
> **Malcolm X**

To these people, the teachings of Malcolm X and the Nation of Islam made a lot of sense. Why waste their time and risk their lives trying to ride buses with white people or enroll in white people's colleges? Why bother voting in racist elections? Perhaps their energies would be better spent improving their own communities and not integrating with white people at all.

CONNECT

Listen to Malcolm X address an assembly in Harlem in New York City in 1964. Why does he compare people in Africa to people in the United States?

🔎 **Malcolm X Any Means Necessary**

Many Black Americans continued to live in poverty on Southern plantations or in the ghettoes in the cities. Black men were still beaten by white police officers. Black activists were still killed by white supremacists.

A Change of Heart

Like many others, Malcolm X had been drawn to the Nation of Islam because it offered an alternate path to racial justice in America. By the early 1960s, however, Malcolm X was losing his faith in Elijah Muhammad and the Nation of Islam.

The stage where Malcolm X was shot dead

Credit: Stanley Wolfson, *New York World-Telegram & Sun* staff photographer

Malcolm X broke his ties with the Nation of Islam. He remained a Muslim, though, and continued to help Black Americans attain their rights.

But the Nation of Islam believed in swift and sometimes severe punishment for anyone who strayed from their teachings. On February 21, 1965, members of the Nation of Islam shot Malcolm X dead while he was speaking in New York City.

Since his release from prison in 1952, Malcolm X, who changed his name to Malcolm Shabazz but was still known as Malcolm X, had traveled the world. Those travels opened his eyes to a much grander vision of Islam than the one taught by Elijah Muhammad. On a pilgrimage to the holy city of Mecca, in Saudi Arabia, Malcolm X discovered traditional Islam, a religion that accepts people of all colors.

Malcolm X returned to the United States in 1964 a changed man. He no longer believed in Elijah Muhammad and the Nation of Islam. Not only was racial harmony possible, he said, it was desirable.

Two leaders who, for most of their careers as activists, approached the same problem from radically different perspectives, were shot dead while doing their best to improve the lives of Black people. Is there anything we can learn about how society treats activists that can be applied to the social movements we see today? How can we keep people safe as they do the important work of demanding change?

WONDER WHY?

What lessons can we take from these assassinations?

PROJECT

Speaking Engagements

Compare the speeches of two very different men fighting for the same cause.

Dr. King at the March on
Washington, August 28, 1963

Malcolm X in 1964

Credit: Herman Hiller, *New York World-Telegram & Sun* staff photographer

☮ **Listen to Martin Luther King Jr's last speech, delivered the night before he was murdered.** Respond to the following questions.

🔍 **"I Have Been to the Mountaintop" full speech**

· Why would King choose to live in his current era over all others in history?

· What does King mean when he says "We are all God's children"?

· Why is King not worried about the threats against his life?

☮ **Listen to Malcolm X's "The Ballot or the Bullet" speech."** Respond to the following questions.

🔍 **Malcolm X "The Ballot or the Bullet"**

· Why did Malcolm X say people need to leave their religion at home?

· Why did he want African Americans to start a self-help program?

· Why does he say the U.S. government has failed African Americans?

TEXT TO WORLD

How is the decentralized leadership approach of the Black Lives Matter movement—where no one leader is the face and voice of the people—different?

PROJECT

Portrait of a Leader

Speeches can be a very powerful tool in activism.

☮ **After you have listened to each of the speeches in the previous project, design a portrait of either King or Malcolm X based on what you heard.** You can draw or paint a portrait, or you can create a portrait made up of words and/or other images and symbols.

☮ **Consider the following questions before you begin your artwork.**

· What three words best describe this man?

· What emotions do you feel when you listen to this man talk?

· Is there any humor in the speech?

· How does the audience seem to feel about him?

Word Power!

What vocabulary words did you discover? Can you figure out the meanings of these words? Look in the glossary for help!

assassination, boycott, desegregation, equality, injustice, pilgrimage, retaliate, and unrivaled

Martin Luther King Jr. and Coretta Scott King, 1964

Credit: Herman Hiller, *New York World-Telegram & Sun*

John Lewis, 2006

CHAPTER FOUR

JOHN
LEWIS

FASTFACTS

BIRTH DATE:
February 21, 1940

PLACE OF BIRTH:
Troy, Alabama

AGE AT DEATH:
80

MAJOR ACCOMPLISHMENTS:

- Cofounder of the Nashville Student Movement

- One of the original Freedom Riders

- Chairman of the Student Nonviolent Coordinating Committee

- U.S. Representative from Atlanta, Georgia

John Lewis's parents raised him to work hard and always obey the law. In his mother's eyes, nothing was more disgraceful than being hauled off to jail like a common criminal. So, when the 20-year-old Lewis committed a crime and was put in jail, you might imagine he felt deeply ashamed. But he didn't. He felt proud.

On February 27, 1960, Lewis was arrested for sitting at a whites-only lunch counter at a Woolworth department store in Nashville, Tennessee. His time as a civil rights protestor had begun, and he couldn't have been happier.

Roots

John Lewis was a child of the Deep South. He grew up in Troy, Alabama, working in cotton fields with his brothers and sisters just like Fannie Lou Hamer did. One big difference, however, was that Lewis's parents owned the land they lived and worked on. Land ownership gave the Lewis family a level of security that Hamer's family never had. Safe on his family's farm, Lewis experienced little of the overt, violent racism that scarred other Black children at a young age.

When Lewis was old enough to venture into town, however, he encountered Jim Crow laws. He could watch his favorite Tarzan movies at the theater, but only if he sat in the balcony. He could buy a Coke inside the drug store, but he had to drink it outside. And the biggest insult of all? He wasn't allowed to check out books from the public library.

That was a huge blow to Lewis. He loved to read. Books brought the world to his doorstep. They showed him a world of possibilities beyond a life of cotton.

CIVIL RIGHTS TIMELINE

1940
John Lewis is born in Troy, Alabama.

1957
Lewis attends college at American Baptist Theological Seminary in Nashville, Tennessee.

1960
Lewis helps found the Nashville Student Movement and the first lunch counter sit-ins begin.

1961
Lewis joins the Freedom Rides to integrate interstate buses.

1963
Lewis becomes chairman of the Student Nonviolent Coordinating Committee (SNCC).

1963
Representing SNCC, Lewis delivers a speech at the March on Washington.

Off to Nashville

Segregated high schools were another sore point for Lewis. It stung to know that the white schools had paved roads, sports fields, gymnasiums, lunch rooms, and indoor bathrooms. His all-Black school had none of those things.

John Lewis attended college at American Baptist Theological Seminary in Nashville, Tennessee.

WONDER WHY?

What role do libraries play in society today? What role do they play in the struggle for equality? Do you think that role is different from what it was in the twentieth century?

Lewis was a dedicated student. When cotton harvest season came around, Lewis refused to work in the fields. While his siblings trudged off to work, Lewis found a place to hide, then snuck off to school when the bus arrived.

Lewis wasn't going to stay home on the farm after he graduated high school, either. In 1957, he boarded a bus for Nashville, Tennessee. He was headed to college at American Baptist Theological Seminary to become a Baptist minister.

1964
Lewis and SNCC help coordinate the Mississippi Freedom Summer voter registration drive.

1965
Lewis leads 600 activists from Selma to Montgomery, Alabama, to protest discriminatory voting laws.

1981
Lewis wins election to the Atlanta City Council.

1986
Lewis wins election to the U.S. House of Representatives.

2011
President Barack Obama awards Lewis the Presidential Medal of Freedom, the highest civil honor in the United States.

2013
Lewis is arrested for participating in a sit-in to demand immigration reform in the United States.

2020
Lewis dies from pancreatic cancer and is the first Black lawmaker to lie in state at the U.S. Capitol Rotunda.

Introduction to Nonviolent Civil Disobedience

His first year at college, Lewis concentrated on studying and practicing his preaching. By his sophomore year, however, he was as much a civil rights activist as he was a student.

James Lawson, shown here in 2010, instructed student activists in nonviolent resistance.

He discovered James Lawson (1928–), a political activist who led workshops on nonviolent resistance for social change. Like Martin Luther King Jr. before him, Lewis learned about Henry David Thoreau and Mahatma Gandhi.

> " You have to do more than just not hit back. You have to have no desire to hit back. You have to love that person who's hitting you."
>
> James Lawson

The Nashville students were taught to refrain from the use of violence in practice as well. They spent hours taking turns belittling one another, yelling the most hurtful things they could think of, loud and up close. The young activists even traveled to a civil rights training center called the Highlander Folk School. The Highlander had trained an older generation of civil rights activists, including Dr. King and Rosa Parks. Now, it trained a younger generation.

Direct Action

By early 1960, the number of student activists in Nashville had grown substantially. Under the leadership of Diane Nash (1938–), they formed their own organization, the Nashville Student Movement.

The Nashville students were eager to put into practice the nonviolent techniques they had learned from James Lawson. They got their chance in February, when a series of sit-ins was organized at segregated lunch counters in downtown Nashville. On February 13, 1960, more than 100 students walked into downtown together. Then, they split up into smaller groups to try their luck being served at lunch counters around the city.

That first day, nothing much happened. At each of the department stores, managers closed down the lunch counters and turned off the lights. The students sat for hours in the dark without further incident, then returned to their home base at the First Baptist Church.

> " All my life I'd . . . obeyed the rules. You can't use that library. You can't drink at that fountain. . . . I hated those rules, but I'd always obeyed them. Until now."
>
> **John Lewis**

The same thing happened during their second and third sit-ins. The students, a mixed group of Black and white, were heckled a bit. Otherwise, they were left in peace.

The fourth sit-in, on February 27, 1960, was a different story. By then, white supremacists were losing their patience. The chief of police warned that if students sat at the lunch counters again, they would be arrested. Rumors circulated that white supremacist groups were planning attacks.

Civil rights leaders, including John Lewis, meet with President John F. Kennedy in the Oval Office of the White House after the March on Washington, DC, 1963.

Credit: Warren K. Leffler, *U.S. News & World Report* magazine collection

When students took their seats, they were assaulted almost immediately. At Woolworth, Lewis was hit in the ribs and knocked off his seat. He watched, but did nothing, as a white man put out a lit cigarette on the neck of one of his fellow activists. The students held their ground while all around them white people jeered.

CONNECT

Watch a brief history of the Nashville lunch counter sit-ins. How do you think it felt to be the first to break the color barrier at the lunch counter?

PLEASE NOTE THIS VIDEO CONTAINS VIOLENT SCENES.

🔍 **mccurl project sit-ins**

At other lunch counters, angry whites poured ketchup and mustard over activists' heads. At McClellan's Department Store, Lewis's friend and co-activist, a white man named Paul LaPrad, was pulled off his stool and beaten.

A television film crew caught the ugly encounter at McClellan's on tape. That night, it was broadcast across the nation. For many white Americans, it was one of the first times they'd witnessed the brutality of racism.

Arrest, Jail, Boycott, Change

When the fighting broke out, police arrived and made arrests—but not of the white attackers. They arrested the demonstrators! Altogether, about 80 student protestors, Lewis among them, were arrested and later found guilty of disorderly conduct. Lewis and the others were ordered to pay a small fine or spend 30 days in jail. Many, Lewis included, chose jail rather than pay the fine. That, too, was a form of nonviolent protest.

Meanwhile, the Black community in Nashville stepped up to support the students' actions. They organized a boycott of white downtown businesses, which was so effective that store owners almost immediately began losing money.

THE GREENSBORO SIT-INS

The first student sit-ins to gain national attention took place in Greensboro, North Carolina. On February 1, 1960, four Black students sat at a whites-only counter at Woolworth. The next day, 28 more students joined them. The third day, 300 activists arrived. Inspired by the Greensboro sit-ins, students throughout the country staged sit-ins of their own.

Civil rights leaders **Bayard Rustin, Andrew Young, William Fitts Ryan, James Farmer, and John Lewis**

Credit: Stanley Wolfson, *New York World-Telegram & Sun*

CORE leader James Farmer, shown here in 1965, organized the initial Freedom Rides.

Sit-ins and the boycott continued through April, when business owners finally threw in the towel. On May 10, 1960, Nashville became the first major city in the United States to integrate its lunch counters.

" These young men and women had no guns with which to defend themselves—no weapons at all, except those of the indomitable human spirit."

James Farmer (1920–1999), civil rights activist

Freedom Riders

Even after the violence he'd seen and experienced, John Lewis still believed in the power of nonviolent, direct action. In the spring of 1961, however, that faith would be tested in far more perilous situations than those he had faced in Nashville.

In 1960, federal laws already made it illegal for interstate buses and bus stations to be racially segregated. But in the South, those laws were ignored. So, in 1961, a civil rights organization known as Congress of Racial Equality (CORE) decided to force the issue. Members organized and trained 13 Black and white activists, Lewis among them, to ride Southern buses together, sit in one another's waiting areas, and use one another's restrooms.

Calling themselves Freedom Riders, they planned a two-week trip. They would leave Washington, DC, on May 4 and arrive in New Orleans, Louisiana, on May 17.

Road Rage

Dr. Martin Luther King Jr. warned one participant that they would "never make it through Alabama." And he was nearly right.

CONNECT

Watch the trailer for a documentary on the Freedom Riders. Can you imagine this happening today?

PLEASE BE AWARE THIS VIDEO CONTAINS DISTURBING IMAGERY AND LANGUAGE.

🔍 Freedom Riders trailer

When the Freedom Riders hit Alabama, they were met with a level of violence that none of them had experienced before. In Anniston, Alabama, a white mob forced one of the buses to the side of the highway and tossed a firebomb into the vehicle. While the bus burned, they blocked the doors so that the passengers could not escape.

When the Freedom Riders did manage to get out, they staggered to the ground and were beaten.

WONDER WHY?

When violence erupted during protests, white mobs frequently attacked white activists more harshly than they did Black activists. Why do you think white activists made attackers so angry?

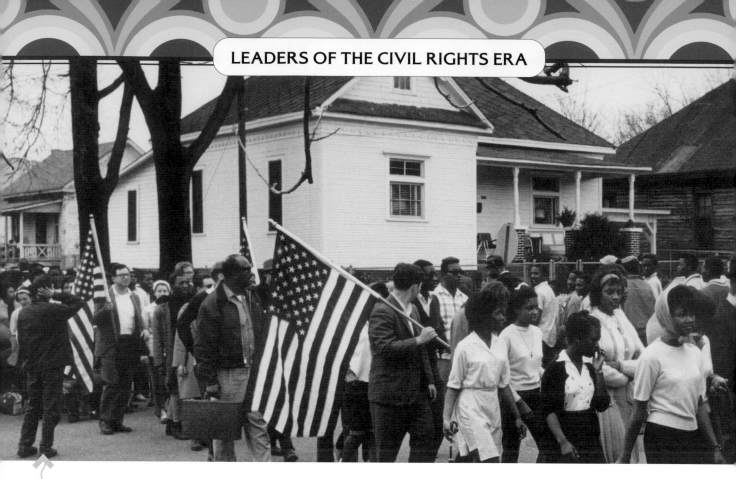

The March from Selma to Montgomery, known as "Bloody Sunday"

Credit: Peter Pettus

In bus stations in both Birmingham and Montgomery, Alabama, white mobs attacked Freedom Riders with baseball bats and iron pipes. In Montgomery, Lewis watched in horror as white journalists were beaten senseless with their own cameras. His friend and co-activist, Jim Zwerg (1939–), was beaten unconscious with a suitcase. Lewis himself passed out when someone hit him over the head with a wooden crate.

Wounded Riders ended up in hospitals. Hundreds ended up in jail. But more activists—Black and white, from the North and the South—arrived to take their place. President Kennedy asked for a "cooling off period." But the students refused to quit, regardless of the danger. Even knowing she was pregnant, leader Diane Nash joined the action and spent time in jail.

The Freedom Rides continued into September. Eventually, 60 different Freedom Rides took place throughout the country.

CONNECT

You can see pictures of John Lewis joining President Obama and thousands of others to commemorate Bloody Sunday 50 years later.

🔍 **Selma, 50 Years Later**

Lewis served as SNCC's chairman for two tumultuous years. He repeatedly found himself at the center of some of the most important civil rights protests of the entire movement.

Lewis was a speaker at the March on Washington. He worked side by side with Fannie Lou Hamer in Mississippi during the Freedom Summer campaign. He was among the activists who demanded the MFDP be recognized at the Democratic National Convention in Atlantic City, New Jersey.

CONNECT

Listen to Lewis's speech at the March on Washington.

🔍 John Lewis speech March Washington

In November 1961, the federal government established new rules that prohibited segregation on public buses. This time, those laws were enforced—even in the South.

Leading the SNCC

The year 1963 saw John Lewis working fulltime as a civil rights activist. He was the new chairman of the Student Nonviolent Coordinating Committee (SNCC). SNCC (or *snick*, as it was pronounced) had formed in 1961 during the first college student lunch counter sit-ins.

Lewis also marched at the front of hundreds of activists as they walked from Selma to Montgomery, Alabama, to demand voting rights for Black people. This protest became known as Bloody Sunday because state troopers and others brutally attacked the peaceful protestors. When Lewis crossed the Edmund Pettis Bridge, a white state trooper fractured his skull with a nightstick.

Lewis could quietly handle the violence directed at himself, but when it was turned on the people he recruited and trained in SNCC, it troubled him a great deal. That was certainly the case in Mississippi during Freedom Summer of 1964.

FAMILY FACTS

Lewis married Lillian Miles (1939–2012) in 1968. They had one son, John Miles Lewis.

Lewis knew that demanding racial justice in Mississippi was dangerous. The mayor of Jackson, Mississippi, prepared for the summer campaign by stockpiling an additional 200 shotguns and buying an Army tank and extra tear gas. The KKK prepared by burning crosses in 64 of Mississippi's 82 counties—in just one night.

But this knowledge didn't prepare him for when three SNCC activists went out to register voters and were later found dead in an earthen dam. The three young men—Michael Schwerner (1939–1964) and Andrew Goodman (1943–1964), both white and from the North, and James Chaney (1943–1964), a Black Mississippian—had been beaten and shot to death.

Of the Freedom Summer of 1964, Lewis said: "No one who went into Mississippi that summer came out the same . . . . [They] came out of that summer wounded, literally and emotionally."

Working from the Inside

When Lewis first became active in the Civil Rights Movement, he was studying to become a minister. After graduation, however, Lewis became a politician.

He won election to the Atlanta City Council in 1981 and then was elected to represent the state of Georgia in the U.S. Congress in 1986. He was re-elected to the U.S. House of Representatives 16 times.

Civil rights leaders Dr. Ralph David Abernathy and Dr. and Mrs. Martin Luther King Jr. march with the Abernathy children on the front line, leading the Selma to Montgomery March in 1965.

Credit: Abernathy family

Protestors with the Mississippi Freedom Democratic Party hold up signs with pictures of James Chaney, Andrew Goodman, and Michael Schwerner.

Credit: Warren K. Leffler, *U.S. News & World Report* magazine collection

Being an elected official, however, never stopped Lewis from taking direct, nonviolent action against injustice. In 2006 and 2009, he was arrested for protesting genocide in Sudan. He was arrested again in 2013 for his participation in a sit-in to demand immigration reform in the United States.

Lewis helped a nation grow into one that is far more equal than it was previously, and he did so without inflicting violence. Not only that, he taught scores of other people how to handle themselves when faced with brutality. His lessons will help guide protestors for as long as there is activism.

Marchers in Harlem, New York

Credit: Stanley Wolfson, *New York World-Telegram & Sun*

PROJECT

At the Museum

Rep. John Lewis helped pass the bill that resulted in the construction of the National Museum of African American History and Culture (NMAAHC). It opened in Washington, DC, in 2016.

 **Explore the NMAAHC website and take the digital tour.** Then create a poster collage about the museum. Use the following questions to guide your work.

🔍 NMAAHC

- Describe some of the topics that the museum explores. How many different subject areas can you find?

- What temporary exhibit is currently on display? When will that exhibit close? Would you like to see it? Why or why not?

- Which exhibit would you most like to see? Why?

- Does anything about the museum surprise you? Why or why not?

Tour the NMAAHC.

🔍 tour NMAAHC

Explore the websites of museums that highlight the history of other oppressed groups, such as the U.S. Holocaust Memorial Museum or the National Museum of the American Indian in Washington, DC.

- What are some of the issues that these museums highlight?

- What do you learn from them?

- Why is it important to have spaces that focus on different groups?

- What other museums would you like to see developed?

TEXT TO WORLD

Do you think you would be able to maintain a peaceful protest if people began to turn violent toward you? What strategies might work to keep you calm and focused?

PROJECT

How to be an Anti-Racist

The Civil Rights Movement improved many aspects of American society. Unfortunately, racism itself still exists. In the year 2020, many Americans were concerned about ongoing racial inequalities in the United States. They began to question what they as individuals could do to promote racial harmony. A new goal—becoming anti-racist—is now part of the American conversation about race.

✌ **Read the questions provided below.** Then, watch at least the first 20 minutes of the YouTube conversation between Sherice Torres and Ibram X. Kendi (1982-) as they discuss anti-racism.

· How is denial a key element of racism?

· Why does Kendi point out a difference between changing people's behavior and changing who people are?

· Kendi says people can change racist behavior if they confess they have done something wrong, recognize they made a mistake, and decide to make a change. Do you agree that people can change their racist behaviors?

· What is the difference between "policy" and "people" that Kendi talks about? What is the difference between a "dangerous Black neighborhood" and a "dangerous poor neighborhood"?

✌ **Can you can list three things you as an individual might do to create more racial equity in your community?**

CONNECT

Listen to the discussion on anti-racism.

🔍 Toores Kendi

What vocabulary words did you discover? Can you figure out the meanings of these words? Look in the glossary for help!

brutality, discrimination, disorderly conduct, genocide, heckle, jeer, nonviolent protest, perilous, and segregate

A mural in Philadelphia by artist Parris Stancell, sponsored by the Freedom School Mural Arts Program. Left to right; Malcolm X, Ella Baker, Martin Luther King Jr., Frederick Douglass

Credit: Tony Fischer (CC BY 2.0)

CHAPTER FIVE

ELLA
BAKER

FASTFACTS

BIRTH DATE:
December 13, 1903

PLACE OF BIRTH:
Norfolk, Virginia

AGE AT DEATH:
83

MAJOR ACCOMPLISHMENTS:

- Field secretary for the NAACP

- Associate director of the SCLC

- Organizer and mentor for SNCC

By the time Ella Baker was 57, she had been an activist in the Civil Rights Movement for decades. She had been the highest ranking female staff member of the NAACP. She was the current interim director of the SCLC.

8th Annual
Youth Conference

NEW ORLEANS LOUISIANA

NOV. 21-24 1946

N.A.A.C.P. 20 WEST 40th STREET NEW YORK 18, N. Y.

Now, during Easter break in 1960, Baker gathered together hundreds of Black college activists who had been staging lunch counter sit-ins all over the South. Under her guidance, the students formed a new organization— the Student Nonviolent Coordinating Committee (SNCC). Before the students returned to their colleges, Baker gave them some advice. Be wary, she said, of "leader-centered orientation."

Everyone knew what she meant. Student activist Julian Bond (1940–2015) summed it up perfectly: "Don't let Martin Luther King Jr. tell you what to do." Baker was a staunch believer in the power of grassroots organizing.

Baker would spend the remainder of her life teaching people how to organize among themselves as a group.

A poster for the NAACP youth conference, 1946

CIVIL RIGHTS TIMELINE

1903
Ella Baker is born in Norfolk, Virginia.

1927
Baker graduates from Shaw University and moves to Harlem, New York.

1940
Baker becomes a field secretary for the national office of the NAACP.

1946
Baker leaves the national NAACP. She works in local civil rights groups in Harlem.

Roots

Ella Baker grew up largely sheltered from the harshest realities that Black people faced in the Jim Crow South. She was born in Norfolk, Virginia, and lived there until she was seven years old. After race riots broke out in Norfolk in 1910, Ella's mother, Anna Ross Baker, relocated the family to her hometown of Littleton, North Carolina.

> "Strong people don't need strong leaders."
>
> Ella Baker

Ella's father, Blake Baker, continued to work for a steamship line that sailed out of Norfolk. This arrangement separated the family for weeks at a time. But that was a sacrifice the Bakers were willing to make if it shielded their children from racial violence.

Shaw Academy and University

Ella Baker's family was not financially well off. Nonetheless, they enjoyed a lifestyle in Littleton that placed them among the "elite" of their race. They lived in a relatively spacious, six-room rented house. Ella took piano lessons and never missed a day of school working in a cotton field.

THE FIGHT OF THE CENTURY

On July 4, 1910, heavyweight boxer Jack Johnson (1878–1946), a Black man, defeated heavyweight champion James Jeffries (1875–1953), a white man, to win the title. The contest became known as "the fight of the century," in part because it stirred up racial tensions all across the United States. After the contest, race riots broke out in more than 25 states and 50 cities, including Norfolk, Virginia.

Jack Johnson, right, battles James Jeffries in the "fight of the century."

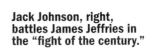

1957
Baker works as an administrator and organizer for the SCLC.

1960
Baker helps form SNCC. She leaves her paid job at SCLC.

1963
Baker becomes a key volunteer organizer and mentor to SNCC students.

1986
Baker dies on her 83rd birthday.

Baker attended a boarding school associated with Shaw University in Raleigh, North Carolina, then received her bachelor's degree from the university in 1927.

WONDER WHY?

How might Baker's upbringing give her a different perspective from the civil rights leaders who grew up in poverty?

Most impressive of all, Ella attended high school at the all-Black Shaw Academy boarding school in Raleigh, North Carolina. There, Baker received an education that was superior to that of nearly any white student in the country.

After graduating high school, Baker stayed on in Raleigh and attended college at Shaw University. She gained a reputation as a gifted public speaker, and she honed her journalism skills by becoming both a writer and an editor of school publications.

When Baker graduated in April 1927, she was class valedictorian and one of two students to give an address at the graduation ceremony.

Getting Started

Ella Baker's mother had hoped her daughter would become a teacher. But Baker had other plans. She wanted a career where she helped bring about social and economic justice for African Americans. That was her dream.

CONNECT

Listen to Ella Baker give a speech at the 1974 Puerto Rico solidarity rally. Why does she say the struggle has to be made every day?

 Baker struggle every day

After graduating college, Baker moved to the Black neighborhood of Harlem in New York City. She had her sights set on working at the national offices of the NAACP.

That proved harder than Baker had anticipated. Thirteen years passed before she was hired as a field secretary for the NAACP. Once she arrived, however, Baker made her mark.

As a field secretary, Baker's job was to bring in new members and develop the NAACP from the ground up. No one was better at this than Baker. Traveling throughout the South, she forged strong personal bonds with rank-and-file NAACP members everywhere she went. Other field secretaries dropped into town, delivered a speech, and left. Baker stayed for days or weeks, and she went straight to the people. She visited barbershops, bars, pool halls, shipyards, and beauty salons—anyplace where she could connect with working-class Black Americans.

An NAACP promotional poster from 1946

SHAW UNIVERSITY

Ella Baker was educated at Shaw University, a school founded in 1865 by a white Baptist minister named Henry Martin Tupper (1831–1893). Tupper had once planned to do missionary work in Africa. But when the Civil War ended, he decided instead to focus his missionary work on assisting the South's newly freed Black Americans. Shaw University has the distinction of being the first university devoted to the education of Black Americans after the Civil War. Fortunately for Ella Baker, it is one of the oldest coeducational universities in the country as well.

In the six years that Baker worked for the NAACP, from 1940 to 1946, membership numbers grew from 50,000 to 450,000. Baker didn't build that network on her own, of course. But she set the standard for what field secretaries could accomplish.

Finding the Right Fit

Working for the NAACP had been a dream come true for Baker, yet she left the organization after just six years. She found her next major civil rights job in 1957, when she worked for the newly formed Southern Christian Leadership Conference (SCLC), headed by Martin Luther King Jr. She stayed with the SCLC for just three years.

> " I am not white. There is nothing within my mind and heart which tempts me to think I am."
>
> **Walter White,** a Black civil rights activist whose ancestors included slave owners

Walter White was head of the NAACP while Baker was a field secretary.

Why did Baker leave jobs with the preeminent organizations of the Civil Rights Movement? From her point of view, the NAACP and the SCLC were doing things backward. They were "top-down" organizations. Directives came from the top, from people such as executive secretary Walter White (1893–1955) at the NAACP or Dr. King at the SCLC. Baker thought that system needed to be reversed; directives should come from the ground up. She believed that the real power of the movement resided in networks of strong local leaders. The national groups should follow *their* lead, not the other way around.

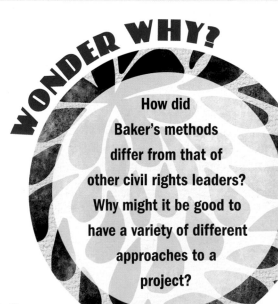

WONDER WHY? How did Baker's methods differ from that of other civil rights leaders? Why might it be good to have a variety of different approaches to a project?

A White House meeting with civil rights leaders, including Martin Luther King Jr.

Mentoring the Next Generation

As Baker watched Dr. King's fame increase, she became even more uncomfortable with a top-down approach to achieving racial justice. Hero worship, she feared, made the movement weaker, not stronger. It was why she warned the students of SNCC to stay clear of a "leader-centered orientation." It was also why she left the SCLC and focused her efforts on developing the next generation of leaders.

WONDER WHY?

Do you think social change comes from the top down or the ground up? Is it perhaps a combination of both? Which method have other civil rights movements used?

91

Throughout the 1960s, Baker became a vital behind-the-scenes mentor and organizer to the college students of SNCC. SNCC centered much of its early activism in rural Mississippi, where devotion to Jim Crow ran so deep that other organizations backed away from the state altogether.

Andrew Young (1932–), of the SCLC, described Mississippi as the "depths of depravity of Southern racism. We knew better," he said, "than to try to take on Mississippi."

The students, apparently, did not "know better." Under Baker's guidance, SNCC tackled racism in Mississippi head-on. And they did it Baker's way, by going directly to the people at the lowest rungs of the social ladder. They knocked on the doors of sharecroppers. They walked into the cotton fields where Black people worked. They visited the barbershops and the beauty salons where Black people felt free to share their opinions, their fears, their hopes and dreams.

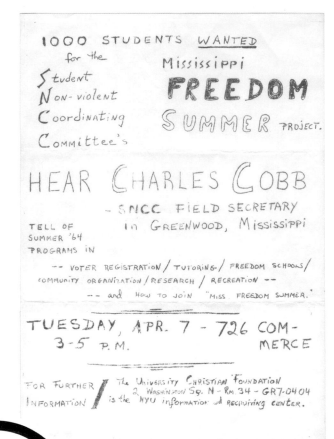

CONNECT

Listen to Cornell West speak about Baker as a leader. How were her views on leadership a strength? How might she have viewed the Black Lives Matter movement, with its decentralized leadership approach?

🔍 **Cornell West Ella Baker**

Student Activism

With a goal of empowering poor and illiterate Black people in Mississippi, Baker guided SNCC activists in a series of innovative programs.

Baker was behind SNCC's involvement in a series of events called Freedom Days. These were organized drives to register Black voters, such as the one that took place in Hattiesburg, Mississippi, on January 22, 1964.

Signs in a field in Mississippi during Freedom Summer

Credit: Thomas Foner, courtesy of the Mississippi Department of Archives and History

Baker was on hand, as was Fannie Lou Hamer, offering support to 150 Black men and women brave enough to attempt to register to vote.

Like Hamer before them, few succeeded in their first attempts. Nonetheless, the sight of 150 Black people peacefully demanding their right to do so was a landmark event in Mississippi.

That summer of 1964, Baker and SNCC also participated in the statewide voter registration drive called Freedom Summer. Baker, like Hamer and their protégé, John Lewis, had hoped an influx of white college students from the North would broaden the appeal of civil rights activism in Mississippi. Like her fellow activists, Baker was also crushed by the murders of James Chaney, Michael Schwerner, and Andrew Goodman.

> " **Freedom, by definition, is people realizing that they are their own leaders.**"
>
> Diane Nash (1938–)

MOCK VOTE

SNCC members were active in the Freedom Vote of 1963, a mock election for governor and lieutenant governor of Mississippi. White supremacists argued that Black people could vote in Mississippi, they just chose not to. Working with local leaders such as Fannie Lou Hamer, SNCC helped collect the ballots of more than 80,000 Black Mississippians. The votes weren't real, but they proved a point. Black Mississippians would vote if they could do so without fear of losing their jobs or being terrorized by white supremacists.

Had the more conservative organizations been correct? Was it too dangerous to push for change in Mississippi? Baker guided the students to answer those questions to their own satisfaction. And they always came back resolved not to back down in the face of violent resistance.

WONDER WHY?

Was it a mistake for Ella Baker and SNCC to go into Mississippi? Should they have stayed away? Why or why not?

The car from which the three activists went missing on June 21, 1964, sparked a massive search.

Credit: Federal Bureau of Investigation

The students having made up their own minds, Baker backed them up. She was always there, behind the scenes, finding safe houses and hotels for them to stay in. Wherever they went, she hooked them up with local activists. She took their phone calls in the middle of the night. She wrote long letters to them, supporting them with the wisdom of her many years of experience. They talked with her individually on a near daily basis. And when they gathered for conferences, Baker's speeches inspired them to continue their quest for justice. Said historian Howard Zinn (1922–2010), Ella Baker was "more responsible than any other single individual for the formation of the new abolitionists."

FAMILY FACTS

Ella Baker was married to her college sweetheart, T.J. Roberts, for 20 years. Unusual for her time, Baker chose not to take her husband's last name, nor did she choose to have children.

Ella Baker became a legend of the Civil Rights Movement, as did Martin Luther King Jr., Malcolm X, Fannie Lou Hamer, and John Lewis. They were a diverse group of people. Some grew up in relative comfort. Some lived the hard lives of sharecroppers. One was even a convicted felon. But they all had one thing in common: They were committed to the cause of equal justice for African Americans.

> "[W]e are not fighting for the freedom of the Negro alone, but for . . . a larger freedom that encompasses all of mankind."
>
> **Ella Baker**

That cause is just as crucial today as it was during the Civil Rights Movement. The Black Lives Matter movement, sparked in part by the killings of African Americans at the hands of police, has brought the fight for racial equality back to the forefront of America's attention.

As you read the news and watch the videos, try to identify the leaders of this wave of protest. Who are they? Where are they communicating their thoughts? What actions are they taking to change how people think and behave? And how can you do the work to support anti-racism?

THE TALENTED TENTH

Ella Baker's conviction that poor, illiterate, Black Americans could develop their own strategies for gaining equality put her at odds with many people in the Civil Rights Movement. The Black scholar W.E.B. Du Bois had argued that the Black race would only be saved by what he called the "talented tenth." That is, the Black race's salvation resided in the one in 10 Black men who graduated from college and enjoyed a middle class lifestyle. Many Black Americans agreed with Du Bois that these "elites" were the only people capable of guiding the movement. Baker strongly disagreed. Given the proper support, Baker believed that all people could find solutions to their problems.

What vocabulary words did you discover? Can you figure out the meanings of these words? Look in the glossary for help!

anti-racism, forge, influx, interim, mentor, mock, preeminent, protégé, rank and file, resolved, wary, and valedictorian

PROJECT

Student Leaders

One thing Ella Baker was known for was teaching and supporting younger people as they learned to fight for equal rights. Why was this an important part of the Civil Rights Movement? Are young people today encouraged to be activists?

☮ **Ella Baker mentored the six student leaders listed below.**

Female Leaders:
- Diane Nash
- Ruby Doris Robinson
- Jean Wheeler Smith

Male Leaders:
- James Bevel
- Robert Moses
- Stokely Carmichael

☮ **Choose the name of one woman and one man and explore their careers in the movement.** Create a poster that includes a photograph of each person and lists some of their career highlights. These questions can guide your research.

- When and where were they born?
- Which college did they attend?
- Did they hold elected positions within SNCC?
- What protests or campaigns did they participate in?

CONNECT

Listen to "Ella's Song," performed by Sweet Honey in the Rock. What role did music play in the Civil Rights Movement?

🔍 Ella's Song Sweet Honey

TEXT TO WORLD

Why do younger people sometimes take risks where older people do not? Do you think this is still true today? Are the people taking part in protests around the world—about climate, racial equality, or police brutality—usually younger or older?

PROJECT

The Harlem Renaissance

As a young woman, Ella Baker lived in Harlem during a time known as the "Harlem Renaissance." This was a time when artists, writers, thinkers, musicians, and other types of creatives began to gather and speak in the Harlem, New York, area, launching an intellectual movement based in the African American experience.

Jazz was a major part of the Harlem Renaissance.

Credit: William Gottlieb

☮ **Watch the following 30-minute documentary about The Harlem Renaissance.**

🔍 **From These Roots: Harlem Renaissance**

☮ **List three ways that this time period influenced American culture.** Use the following questions to guide your thinking.

· What made the Harlem Renaissance revolutionary?

· What is the connection between creative lives and activism?

· Was there much overlap for people in terms of their creative pursuits and their political views?

☮ **Compare your list with others.** Did you all come up with the same things?

CONNECT

Watch a student documentary about Ella Baker. Why is she still interesting to students of today?

🔍 **Leone-Getten Ella Baker**

abolish: to completely put an end to something.

abolitionist: an activist who works to organize to end slavery.

activist: a person who fights for something they believe in.

ally: a partner in an alliance.

alternate: a different option or opportunity.

amendment: an article added to the U.S. Constitution.

ancestor: a person from your family or culture who lived before you.

anti-racism: opposing racism and promoting racial tolerance.

assassination: murder committed for political rather than personal reasons.

assault: a violent physical or verbal attack.

belittle: to make fun of.

bias: prejudice in favor of or against something or someone.

blackface: dark makeup worn (as by a performer) in a caricature of the appearance of a Black person.

boycott: to refuse to buy certain goods or use certain services as a form of protest.

brutality: great physical and mental cruelty.

burglary: entering a building in order to steal.

citizen: a person who has all the rights and responsibilities that come with being a full member of a country.

Civil Rights Movement: a national movement for racial equality in the 1950s and 1960s.

civil rights: the basic rights that all citizens of a society are supposed to have, such as the right to vote.

colonist: a new settler in an area who is originally from somewhere else.

constitution: the basic principles and laws of a nation or state that determine the powers and duties of the government and guarantees certain rights to the people in it.

convicted: found guilty of having committed a crime.

convictions: guilty verdicts in a court of law.

culture: a group of people and their beliefs and way of life.

current events: important events that are happening in the world.

de facto: a fact, whether or not it's right or ethical.

debate: to argue about something, trying to convince the other person of a point of view.

debt: a service or money owed.

decentralized leadership: in an organization, when the group is steered by all of the members instead of one or two clear leaders.

defense attorney: a lawyer who represents people accused of crimes in a court of law.

delegate: a person sent to a political event to represent others.

depravity: wickedness.

desegregate: to end segregation.

discrimination: the unjust treatment of some groups of people based on factors such as their race, religion, or gender.

disorderly conduct: behavior that disturbs the people gathered in a public space.

diverse: having a wide variety of characteristics.

eligible: able to be chosen for something.

elite: set aside for a chosen few.

GLOSSARY

environmental: relating to the natural world and the impact of human activity on its condition.

equality: being the same in power and status.

farce: an empty or ridiculous act.

feminist: a person who believes men and women should have equal rights and opportunities.

forge: to create a strong relationship.

freedom: the ability to choose and act without constraints.

galvanize: to shock or excite someone into taking action.

gender: the behavioral, cultural, or psychological traits typically associated with masculinity and femininity.

genocide: the destruction of an entire group of people.

ghetto: a section of a city, often rundown, in which primarily members of minority groups live because of social, legal, or economic pressure.

gospel music: Christian music, most closely associated with Black American churches.

grassroots: an organization made up of many ordinary people.

heckle: to make rude or abusive comments to a person trying to speak.

hero worship: to think highly of someone as a hero to the point of ignoring any detriments.

hone: to sharpen and improve one's skills.

hypocrisy: behaving in a way that contradicts what you claim to believe or feel.

ideal: a standard or belief that people strive to achieve.

ideology: a set of opinions or beliefs.

illiterate: not being able to read or write.

immigration: moving to a new country to live there.

immune: the ability of a person to resist.

impartial: fair, without bias or prejudice.

inequity: the fact of being unfair, or an unfair situation.

inferior: lower in rank, status, or quality.

influx: the arrival of a large number of people or things.

injustice: unfair action or treatment.

innovative: coming up with new ideas or methods of doing things.

integrate: desegregating, or bringing together people of all races or ethnic groups in schools, workplaces, and neighborhoods.

interim: in between.

interstate: passing from one state to another, such as going from Louisiana to Mississippi.

intrepid: fearless or adventurous.

irrepressible: unable to be stopped.

Islam: the religious faith of Muslims, including belief in Allah as the sole deity and in Muhammad as his prophet.

jeer: to make rude or mocking remarks.

Jim Crow: the legally enforced discrimination of Black people that led to the practice of segregating African Americans in the United States.

juror: someone who is part of a jury.

justice: fair treatment.

Ku Klux Klan (KKK): a terrorist group formed after the Civil War that believes white Christians should hold the power in society. It uses violence against African Americans and other minority groups.

legitimate: following the laws or rules.

liberate: to set someone free, especially from slavery or imprisonment.

literacy: the ability to read and write.

lucrative: making a great deal of money or profit.

lynching: to kill a person without legal authority, usually by hanging.

menial: boring work that does not require skill and pays very little money.

mentor: an older, more experienced person who guides a younger person in a career.

mock: make believe or fake.

momentum: forward movement, picking up speed.

moral: ethical and honest behavior.

Muslim: a person who follows the religion of Islam.

NAACP: the National Association for the Advancement of Colored People, a group formed during the early twentieth century to advance justice for African Americans.

nationalism: an extreme form of patriotism, especially marked by excessive or undiscriminating devotion to country.

nightstick: a club carried and used by police officers.

nonviolent protest: the practice of achieving goals such as social change through symbolic protests, civil disobedience, economic noncooperation, or other methods, all while being nonviolent.

obligation: a duty, something a person is required to do.

obstacle: something that blocks a person's way or stops progress.

offensive: causing someone to feel deeply hurt, upset, or angry.

oppress: to use unjust or cruel authority and power to persecute someone.

orientation: the manner in which an object or organization is situated.

overt racism: racism that is intentional and usually very recognizable.

parasite: a living thing that feeds off another living thing.

pawn: to give a valuable item to a shopkeeper in exchange for money.

perilous: full of danger or risk.

pilgrimage: a journey to a religious site.

poll tax: a fee that must be paid before you are allowed to vote.

porter: a servant on a railroad car.

preeminent: the very best, of highest quality.

prohibit: to make illegal.

prosecutor: a lawyer who represents the government in court.

protégé: a person who is guided by someone older and more experienced.

race: a group of people of common ancestry who share certain physical characteristics such as skin color.

racism: negative opinions or treatment of people based on race and the notion that people of a different race are inferior because of their race.

racist: hatred of people of a different race.

rank and file: the ordinary members of an organization.

recruit: to convince a person or group to assist or help.

refrain: to keep from doing something.

reign of terror: a historic period of bloodshed and fear.

repercussion: the effect or result of an event or action.

representative: an elected official who acts on behalf of the community that elected them.

reside: to belong by right to a person, group of people, or place.

resolve: to find a solution to a problem or to commit to something.

retaliate: to fight back.

revolutionary: causing a dramatic change.

righteousness: being morally right or justified.

riot: a gathering of people that gets out of control and violent.

sacrifice: to give something up for the sake of something else.

scrutiny: close examination.

segregate: to separate people based on race, religion, ethnicity, or some other category.

segregation: the enforced separation of different racial groups in a community or country.

servitude: to be in service of someone.

sharecropper: a farmer who works on someone else's land and receives a small share of a crop's value after paying for tools, seeds, housing, and food.

sit-in: a form of protest in which people occupy a space and refuse to move.

slave: a person considered the legal property of another and forced to work without pay and against their will.

slum: a crowded area of a city where poor people live and buildings are in bad condition.

social change: a change in social behavior, patterns, and values through time.

spokesperson: someone who speaks for a group.

suffragist: a person advocating for the right of women especially and other groups to vote.

tactic: a carefully planned action or strategy to achieve something.

tenant farmer: a person who farms rented land.

terror: violence or the threat of violence used as a weapon of intimidation.

tumultuous: excited, confused, or disorderly.

unbiased: not having formed an opinion before you have considered all the evidence presented in court.

unconstitutional: not in agreement or accordance with a political constitution, especially the U.S. Constitution.

unjust: something that is unfair.

unrest: a disturbed or uneasy state.

unrivaled: better than anyone or anything else.

urban: relating to a city or large town.

valedictorian: the highest achieving student of a graduating class.

verdict: a legal decision made by a judge or jury.

voter literacy test: a test you have to take and pass in order to be allowed to vote, used during the Jim Crow era to prevent Black people from participating in democracy.

wary: cautious.

white supremacy: the racist belief that white people are superior to those of all other races and should therefore dominate society.

RESOURCES

MUSEUMS

Birmingham Civil Rights Institute, Birmingham, Alabama, bcri.org

Freedom Rides Museum, Montgomery, Alabama, ahc.alabama.gov/properties/freedomrides/freedomrides.aspx

International Civil Rights Museum & Center, Greensboro, North Carolina, sitinmovement.org

The King Center, Atlanta, Georgia, thekingcenter.org/plan-your-visit

The Legacy Museum: From Enslavement to Mass Incarceration,
Montgomery, Alabama, museumandmemorial.eji.org

The Martin Luther King, Jr. National Historical Park, Atlanta, Georgia, nps.gov/malu/index.htm

The National Civil Rights Museum at the Lorraine Motel, Memphis, Tennessee, civilrightsmuseum.org

MONUMENTS & MEMORIALS

Birmingham Civil Rights National Monument, Birmingham, Alabama, nps.gov/bicr/index.htm

Civil Rights Memorial, Montgomery, Alabama, splcenter.org/civil-rights-memorial

Malcolm X Memorial Foundation, Omaha, Nebraska, malcolmxfoundation.org

The National Memorial for Peace and Justice, Montgomery, Alabama, museumandmemorial.eji.org

Thurgood Marshall Memorial, Annapolis, Maryland, visitmaryland.org/listing/general-attractions/
thurgood-marshall-memorial

Virginia Civil Rights Memorial, Richmond, Virginia, edu.lva.virginia.gov/online_classroom/
shaping_the_constitution/doc/virginia_civil_rights_memorial

TRAILS

United States Civil Rights Trail, civilrightstrail.com

VIDEOS

Eyes on the Prize: America's Civil Rights Years 1954–1965. PBS. DVD release date 2012.

Fannie Lou Hamer: Voting Rights Activist & Civil Rights Leader.
TMW Media Group, Inc. DVD release date 2010.

John Lewis: Get in the Way. PBS. DVD release date 2017.

King: The Martin Luther King Story. Olive Films. DVD release date 2015.

Malcolm X. Warner Brothers Studios. DVD release date 2005.

Marshall. Universal Pictures Home Entertainment. DVD release date 2018.

Selma. Paramount Studios. DVD release date 2015.

RESOURCES

QR CODE GLOSSARY

PAGE 10: youtube.com/watch?v=URxwe6LPvkM

PAGE 11: climateone.org/video/bridging-gap-between-civil-rights-and-environmental-advocates

PAGE 17: nhpbs.pbslearningmedia.org/resource/bf10.socst.us.global.houston2/charles-hamilton-houston-and-his-legal-challenge-against-jim-crow

PAGE 19: thurgoodmarshall.com/thurgood-marshall-videos

PAGE 21: youtube.com/watch?v=sWuXMjrv4aA

PAGE 22: youtube.com/watch?v=KEjgAXxrkXY

PAGE 30: youtube.com/watch?v=-a3KqhkPQ-s

PAGE 31: youtube.com/watch?v=CxTReRmH2jA

PAGE 33: thirteen.org/wnet/jimcrow/voting_literacy.html

PAGE 37: youtube.com/watch?v=xhiV6DB_h_8

PAGE 39: youtube.com/watch?v=O7PwNVCZCcY

PAGE 42: youtube.com/watch?v=HIGsUXjZA5k&t=24s

PAGE 43: youtube.com/watch?v=Aor6-DkzBJ0

PAGE 43: youtube.com/watch?v=Ld6fAO4idal

PAGE 43: youtube.com/watch?v=ZX3b4-ub8_Y

PAGE 46: youtube.com/watch?v=GO2Er9Sr8P0

PAGE 51: people.howstuffworks.com/jane-elliott.htm

PAGE 52: blackpast.org/african-american-history/speeches-african-american-history/1955-martin-luther-king-jr-montgomery-bus-boycott

PAGE 56: youtube.com/watch?v=ARvrvJV4th4

PAGE 63: youtube.com/watch?v=6_uYWDyYNUg

PAGE 64: youtube.com/watch?v=df5kaol1lCs

PAGE 66: www.youtube.com/watch?v=ixfwGLxRJU8&t=3s

PAGE 66: youtube.com/watch?v=8zLQLUpNGsc

PAGE 74: youtube.com/watch?v=Kzp7GOcIMfl

PAGE 77: youtube.com/watch?v=d8CAKAXR-AM

PAGE 78: obamawhitehouse.archives.gov/realitycheck/blog/2015/03/08/behind-lens-selma-50-years-later

PAGE 79: youtube.com/watch?v=tFs1eTsokJg

PAGE 82: nmaahc.si.edu

PAGE 82: youtube.com/watch?v=Rawck7tJMKY

PAGE 83: youtube.com/watch?v=pEjpbDSoBCA

PAGE 88: youtube.com/watch?v=t96fnyLMihA

PAGE 92: youtube.com/watch?v=omyQ6P2SCzo

PAGE 96: youtube.com/watch?v=U6Uus--gFrc

PAGE 97: youtube.com/watch?v=4-ZEvX8xaL0

PAGE 97: youtube.com/watch?v=68U57yi9F1E

SELECTED BIBLIOGRAPHY

Bracey, Earnest N. *Fannie Lou Hamer: The Life of a Civil Rights Icon.* McFarland & Co., 2011.

Frady, Marshall. *Martin Luther King, Jr.: A Life.* Penguin Books, 2006.

Haygood, Wil. *Showdown: Thurgood Marshall and the Supreme Court Nomination that Changed America.* Alfred A. Knopf, 2015.

Marable, Manning. *Malcolm X: A Life of Reinvention.* Penguin Books, 2012.

Ransby, Barbara. *Ella Baker and the Black Freedom Movement: A Radical Democratic Vision.* The University of North Carolina Press, 2003.

Williams, Juan. *Thurgood Marshall: American Revolutionary.* Three Rivers Press, 1998.

Williams, Juan. *Eyes on the Prize: America's Civil Rights Years, 1954–1965.* Penguin Books, 2013.

INDEX